The Hidden Magic of
Walt Disney World

Over 600 Secrets *of the Magic Kingdom, Epcot,*
Disney's Hollywood Studios, and Animal Kingdom

SUSAN VENESS

Adamsmedia

Avon, Massachusetts

Published by Adams Media, a division of F+W Media, Inc.
57 Littlefield Street, Avon, MA 02322. U.S.A.
www.adamsmedia.com

ISBN 10: 1-60550-063-1
ISBN 13: 978-1-60550-063-8

Printed in the United States of America.

J I H G F E D C B

Library of Congress Cataloging-in-Publication Data
is available from the publisher.

This publication is designed to provide accurate and authoritative information with regard to the subject matter covered. It is sold with the understanding that the publisher is not engaged in rendering legal, accounting,
or other professional advice. If legal advice or other expert assistance is
required, the services of a competent professional person should be sought.
— From a *Declaration of Principles* jointly adopted by a Committee of the
American Bar Association and a Committee of Publishers and Associations

Many of the designations used by manufacturers and sellers to distinguish
their product are claimed as trademarks. Where those designations appear
in this book and Adams Media was aware of a trademark claim, the designations have been printed with initial capital letters.

The following are registered trademarks of The Walt Disney Company:
Adventureland, Audio-Animatronics, Disney's Animal Kingdom Park,
Epcot, Fantasyland, Frontierland, Indiana Jones Epic Stunt Spectacular!,
Magic Kingdom Park, Main Street U.S.A., Mickey Mouse, Tomorrowland,
The Twilight Zone: Tower of-Terror, Walt Disney World. Universal Studios
is a registered trademark of Universal Studios, Inc.

Maps copyright © F+W Media, Inc.

This book is available at quantity discounts for bulk purchases.
For information, please call
1-800-289-0963.

dedication

To my beloved husband, Simon, whose unwavering faith, gentle nudges, and loving encouragement make all things possible. You continually open my eyes to life's magic.

Acknowledgments

I wish to thank Eric Jacobson, senior vice president of Creative at WDI; Rilous Carter, vice president, Hollywood Studios; Sue Bryan, senior show producer, director, WDI; Chrissie Allen, senior show producer, director, WDI; Pam Fisher, Walt Disney Imagineer, senior show writer; Bob Zalk, Walt Disney Imagineer, show producer; Margaret Kerry, reference model for Tinker Bell and owner of *www .TinkerBellTalks.com*; Eddie Sotto of SottoStudios/LA; Steve and Kathy Kirk of Kirk Design Incorporated; Dave Smith, Walt Disney World historian; Geoffrey Pointon and Diego Rivera from Walt Disney World Publicity; and the dozens of Walt Disney World Cast Members who shared their love of the parks so freely and are truly the ultimate hidden gems.

Additionally, I wish to thank Jim Hill of Jim Hill Media, not only for his keen observations but also for his generosity in putting me in contact with key people, and for his humorous commentary that always kept me laughing.

Many thanks also go to John and Vera Veness, Chip and Marirosa Toland, Allan Oakley, Nina Dew, and Debbie Churchill for their invaluable input.

And a very special Thank-You to Kathleen Prelesnik, Eugene Hengesbach, and Benjamin Haass, whose unfailing support, insight, and encouragement are priceless.

Contents

Foreword

Magic flows out of the tricks you don't see. It is the magician's way of weaving what is right in front of your eyes with something subtle, something hidden. It is a blending of your expectation of what *should* happen with the delightful surprise of something far more creative.

Disney magic is even more elusive. Some say it's in the attractions, some say it's in the atmosphere, and some credit the can-do attitude of the Cast Members. But nearly everyone who visits the parks agrees: The magic is there; they just can't quite put their finger on where. And like the magician, Disney's magic also lies in the sleight of hand, the hidden detail.

My first visit to the Magic Kingdom was as a child. While it was great family fun and the delight in exploring a "whole new world" was already apparent, my childlike viewpoint did not see any further than that. It wasn't until my next visit in 1989, that I really understood the magic. Settled in my seat during the pre-show for the Living Seas at Epcot, I was fully immersed in watching the movie about how the seas were formed and what their future might be. When the show ended, a set of doors leading to a ride vehicle, the Sea Cabs, opened with a great, satisfying *whoosh*. I was stunned! There was more to this than a film? I was also going to take a ride? Where would it go?

The answer should have been obvious, considering the fact the pavilion contained the world's largest aquarium. But it wasn't. The park experience was so overwhelming;

it was almost impossible to do more than just allow Disney to move me from one attraction to the next, taking in only what was directly in front of me.

Those open doors with an adventure waiting beyond were a defining moment and began my fascination with Disney's flawless ability to add just a bit more.

My Disney obsession translated into yearly vacations, then as an online Disney travel specialist, ultimately becoming a full-time job as a researcher, professional travel writer, and guidebook coauthor, specializing in Orlando and Walt Disney World.

Ongoing research for the guidebook and other writing deepened my knowledge of (and love for) the parks. The more familiar I became with them, the more I began to look around for the smaller details, and the more I looked around, the more I realized how often the details that seemed hidden were actually right in front of my eyes.

Often, I didn't know what I was looking at. Sometimes I knew what I was looking at, but I didn't know why it had been placed there or what it was for. Things had clearly been done for a reason, and I couldn't bear not knowing what that reason was.

Increasingly, I began to feel the real magic of the parks could be found in the details and it became a personal mission to seek them out. Some jumped right out at me (the lanterns in the window in Liberty Square were clearly a reference to Paul Revere and his midnight ride) while others, like the unexpected For Rent sign in a window, left me totally perplexed.

Curiosity led me to the Internet as a means of adding to what I already knew and of enhancing my ability to appreciate the details. But I quickly became frustrated with the wealth of misinformation poured out as fact. Items I read again and again on various sites and forums ultimately proved not to be correct, or to be correct only in part, once I sought them out in the parks. Many statements put forth as fact were a misinterpretation of what the viewers believed they saw or, worse yet, complete fabrications. It sometimes felt like a slap in the face of the creative forces who had worked so painstakingly to tell the full story. I was determined to seek out the tale as it was intended.

What started as a diversion became a passion, and I began to visit the parks at every opportunity, specifically looking for their hidden gems. I no longer saw the attractions as rides, but instead as opportunities to seek out the details, thus viewing the story in a whole new way, a more complete and satisfying way.

The kernel of an idea formed, and within a short time I began writing and researching in earnest, with an eye toward creating a companion guide to the other Disney writing projects my husband, Simon, and I were already doing.

Further inspiration came in the form of my brother, Chip. As young adults, we had taken a vacation together at Walt Disney World, and although I was already a serious Disney fan, the parks held limited appeal for him. In fact, he was bored. But, in 2006, his wife expressed an interest in visiting Walt Disney World. She had never been, and they had a few days to spare.

We invited them down to our home for a visit and planned a few days at Walt Disney World. Chip was willing, but uninspired. I decided to show him the parks in a whole new light, and as we toured Epcot and Magic Kingdom, I pointed out the wonderful Imagineering jewels scattered all around. We talked about the backstories, we stopped and listened, and he opened his eyes wide.

In a thank-you e-mail, he told me it was the best time he's ever had in the parks, and that everyone should see them from that perspective. I agreed.

Whether you are a die-hard Disney fan, a casual visitor, or a guest who suspects there is more to it but aren't sure where to look, let *The Hidden Magic of Walt Disney World* be your tour guide. Allow it to slow you down long enough for the magic to catch up. It's all there—and now you know where to find it!

Introduction

Allow *The Hidden Magic of Walt Disney World* to be your guide on a journey around the Walt Disney World theme parks. You'll get maximum appreciation for your touring time while seeing everything through wide-open eyes. There is so much more than the obvious large-scale features, and the details supporting much of what you will see are as fascinating as the attractions themselves.

With all things Disney, there is always a fundamental *story* to every element of every park. Walt Disney was a master storyteller, after all, and these are not just rides and shows, they are living tributes to the people he employed to make his dreams come true. Each hidden gem has its own enthralling reason for why it is where it is and how it came into being.

Additionally, there are a whole series of special effects and clever visual artistry that would be a shame to miss but are, indeed, overlooked by most visitors. The multilayered creativity of Main Street U.S.A. in the Magic Kingdom, Epcot's harmonious blending of scientific law and nature's gentle flow, the skillful transitions from one land to another all serve to highlight the way Disney's Imagineers present an all-encompassing story.

From the original 1971 development of the Magic Kingdom to the second park, the EPCOT Center (just called Epcot today), then Disney–MGM Studios (now Disney's Hollywood Studios), and the newest park, Disney's Animal Kingdom, prepare for a tour like no other, with an infinite curiosity and an unending eye for detail.

Let *The Hidden Magic of Walt Disney World* point out the things most people fail to notice. Let it show you how to look and listen for yourself so that you can see the parks through different eyes and gain an appreciation for all the subtleties, the things that truly bring these marvelous creations to life.

More than that, let's journey to the very heart of what sets Disney parks apart from the competition. You will certainly feel the magic of being in Walt Disney World. In fact, by the time you've finished reading, you will know exactly where the magic comes from, how it is created, why things are the way you see them, and the immense attention to detail involved. Not only do the stories, Fascinating Facts, and Imagine That! commentary provide a great way of passing time in the typically long lines, they also help to bring the attractions to life with a genuine sense of the creative thinking and far-reaching imagination that set them up in the first place.

As you move through the parks, from attraction to attraction, you'll find the secrets are listed in the order you will discover them. Some of the text is highlighted in bold, allowing you to find things at a glance, especially useful when you have one of those "Come see what I found!" moments. You won't have to wonder where you found it—just quickly scan the text for the appropriate bolded item.

The parks are dynamic, ever-changing, and let's face it, a little bit quirky at times. You may come upon a bit of hidden magic that is not working on the day you visit (those pesky talking water fountains!), or it may be covered up or relocated during times of construction. Happily, there is usually another secret right around the corner, so press on and enjoy as many as you can find.

Ultimately, *The Hidden Magic of Walt Disney World* becomes the perfect companion with which to tour any of Walt Disney World's splendid theme parks, providing a hands-on guide to so much detail that so many miss. It will open the eyes of park-goers to a new world that's been right in front of them all the time; one they've never noticed, understood, or pondered.

And now, here is the full "slow down and smell the roses" guide, starting where The World began . . . Disney's Magic Kingdom.

The Magic Kingdom

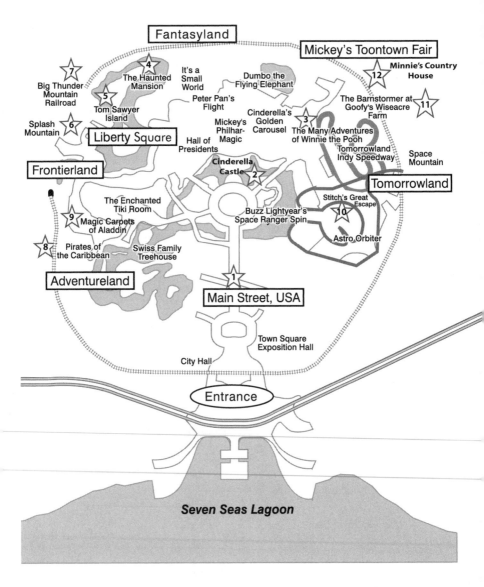

Fantasyland

Mickey's Toontown Fair

Big Thunder Mountain Railroad

The Haunted Mansion

It's a Small World

Dumbo the Flying Elephant

Minnie's Country House

Tom Sawyer Island

Peter Pan's Flight

The Barnstormer at Goofy's Wiseacre Farm

Splash Mountain

Liberty Square

Mickey's Philhar-Magic

Cinderella's Golden Carousel

The Many Adventures of Winnie the Pooh

Frontierland

Hall of Presidents

Cinderella Castle

Tomorrowland Indy Speedway

Space Mountain

The Enchanted Tiki Room

Stitch's Great Escape

Tomorrowland

Magic Carpets of Aladdin

Buzz Lightyear's Space Ranger Spin

Pirates of the Caribbean

Swiss Family Treehouse

Astro Orbiter

Adventureland

Main Street, USA

Town Square Exposition Hall

City Hall

Entrance

Seven Seas Lagoon

The Magic Kingdom

1. Main Street U.S.A.: Notice the smell of home-baked cookies that follows you down Main Street.

2. Cinderella Castle: The three-circled design of the stone fence casts Mickey's silhouette at the right time of day.

3. The Many Adventures of Winnie the Pooh: This attraction took over the location of the beloved Mr. Toad's Wild Ride. Look for the picture of Toad handing Owl the deed to his house.

4. The Haunted Mansion: Ask a Cast Member to tell you the story of Madame Leota's ring.

5. Tom Sawyer Island: Find the paintbrush left by Tom and turn it into a Cast Member. You'll be rewarded with a FastPass for a Frontierland attraction.

6. Splash Mountain: If you decide to watch instead of ride, you might still get wet by a hidden water cannon in the grass!

7. Big Thunder Mountain: Ride at night and you'll see a party in progress in the second-floor window of the saloon.

8. Pirates of the Caribbean: As you exit the ride, look for the distinct footprints of peg-legged Davy Jones.

9. Magic Carpets of Aladdin: Beware of the spitting camels!

10. Stitch's Great Escape: Read the signs written in a peculiar alien alphabet.

11. The Barnstormer at Goofy's Wiseacre Farm: Stand in front of the chicken crates and watch the chickens' reaction as the airplane buzzes by.

12. Minnie's Country House: As you walk through her house, listen to Minnie's answering machine.

Chapter 1

The Magic Kingdom

Touring Disney's Magic Kingdom is like taking a world journey. The park has a distinct flow, from the Small Town America of Walt Disney's childhood memory, to Europe, the New World, the American West, Mexico, the Caribbean, the Middle East, into Space, and finally, to the cartoon world of Walt Disney's imagination.

But there are other ways of looking at the Magic Kingdom as well. We will explore it from three distinct perspectives—the Show, the Facts, and a historical timeline of exploration—giving a sense of the thought and detail that went into creating an all-encompassing world filled with the gentleness of fantasy and the fascination of fact.

Main Street U.S.A.

Every aspect of Walt Disney World focuses on the Show (which invites guests to suspend reality and become part of a fully immersive theatrical experience), but Main Street U.S.A. also tells the Facts about the making of the Magic Kingdom more vividly than any other area of the park. These elements combine seamlessly, creating a sense of Hometown America as Walt Disney remembered it from his childhood home of Marceline, Missouri. Main Street allows guests to feel immediately a sense of familiarity and, at the same time, experience excitement and anticipation for the grand adventure that waits when we venture beyond the boundaries of home.

It all begins when you set foot on Magic Kingdom property. From the perspective of the Show, the turnstiles are like the entry to a grand theater. As you pass under the train station, you see posters representing Coming Attractions, building the excitement for what's in store. Then, walk into the theater, represented by the train station's exit, breathe in the smell of fresh, hot popcorn, and enter the Show. That's when the magic really takes over.

Imagine That!

Walt Disney Imagineering, also known as WDI, is the creative heart of Walt Disney Company, and its wellspring of imagination comes from the people who work there, known as Imagineers (for imagination and engineering). Describing what WDI does, Imagineer Eddie Sotto, senior vice president, Concept Design, who was with WDI from 1986 to 1999, beautifully captures the department's intensity and excitement when he says, "WDI is the perfect storm of imagination, technology, and design that transforms impossible dreams into timeless realities. To me, the thrill ride formula is pretty simple, it's: FEAR MINUS DEATH EQUALS FUN."

Town Square

The best blockbuster movies take your breath away, putting you firmly on the edge of your seat from the very first scene, and Town Square achieves this in high style. Although Cinderella Castle almost pulls you down Main Street, Town Square sets the scene for the experience to come, moving you through Hometown America and out into the World of Walt Disney.

Notice the entire length of Main Street is bordered by red pavement, as if the **Red Carpet** has been rolled out for you. The Fact is, when Kodak was consulted, they determined a particular shade of red enhances guest photographs, especially in direct contrast to the green of the grass.

On the left of Town Square are the town's services, and **Fire Station 71** is a clever nod to 1971, the year the Magic Kingdom opened. On the right are the town's entertainment venues, including Exposition Hall and the local dining hot-spot.

Tony's Town Square, named for the restaurant where **Lady and the Tramp** enjoyed their romantic spaghetti dinner, holds two charming secrets. You will find a tribute to Tramp's love for his beautiful Lady carved into the pavement to the left of the stairs, and if you go inside and walk to the back of the restaurant, you will find them enjoying a quiet meal outside the back window.

Every good Hometown America has its central park, with benches for the townsfolk to relax and enjoy a perfect afternoon. Sit down on the **bench with Goofy**, located in front of City Hall, and he may engage you in conversation.

In the central courtyard, **Roy O. Disney**, Walt's brother and the real driving force behind the Magic Kingdom after Walt passed away in 1966, has his own bench in the park, seated with Minnie Mouse, honoring their supporting roles in the successes of Walt and Mickey.

As you begin to make your way through Town Square, Walt Disney's patriotism shines brightly, with flags flying proudly above each store. To avoid having to take each flag down every night (as required by United States custom), only one flag in all of Main Street U.S.A. is real. The **real flag**, in Town Square, is the one on the main flagpole located in the central courtyard, site of the nightly Flag Lowering Ceremony. Flags printed on banners, T-shirts, underwear, or other clothing are only considered "real" flags if they have the correct number of stars and stripes; and according to United States Code, only real flags are subject to being lowered at dusk.

✳ Fascinating Fact

Though the results of their labors will be appreciated and admired by millions, Imagineers are not allowed to sign their work. Instead, they sometimes place little symbols of themselves, often in the form of initials or birthdates, cleverly disguised to blend into the environment's theme. You will see many as you tour the parks. ✳

Main Street

As you start walking down Main Street, the "movie credits" begin to roll in the **upper windows** above the shops. The window of the first shop on the right-hand side of Main Street, above

Uptown Jewelers, honors the producer, Roy O. Disney. His window reads: *"If We Can Dream It—We Can Do It!" Dreamers and Doers. Roy O. Disney, Chairman.* Walt Disney had the dream, but Roy's financial acumen made that dream come true.

Pay attention to the **streetlamps** down Main Street. They begin as gas lamps near the Emporium, but by the time you reach Casey's Corner restaurant they have progressed to electric lamps. You are symbolically moving through time!

In between Roy's window at the beginning of Main Street and Walt's window at the end are the names of the **cast and crew** who brought the Show to life. Take time to stop and read them to honor these creative men and women.

Main Street's newest window debuted in 2006, just above the Uptown Jewelers. It reads: *"True Tales of Inspiration" Lee A. Cockrell Editor in Chief.* The window honors Mr. Cockrell, editor of the much-enjoyed "Eyes and Ears," the Disney Cast Member newsletter.

Main Street's **second story windows** actually perform a three-part function. At their most basic, they are advertisements for the town's services and business proprietors, from mortgages to dance lessons to interior decorators and so on. As representations of rolling credits, they are the companies involved in creating the Show.

The Fact is, they are the names of the Imagineers, artists, and bogus land-purchasing companies that held instrumental roles in the creation of the Magic Kingdom. Their corresponding businesses allude to the real-life roles they played in the creation of the park. Look for **Big Top Theatrical Productions** *Famous since '55* (developers and designers of many of the New York World's Fair attractions that became Disney classics); **The Camelot Corp.** *Road Show Installation* (show designers); **M. T. Lott Co.** *A Friend in Deeds Is a Friend Indeed* (land acquisition; say the name quickly and you'll get the joke); and **Buena Vista Magic Lantern Slides** *Treat Your Friends to Our Special Tricks* (special effects), among many others. You will find some of these key people in another area of the park, and another bit of hidden magic.

Imagine That!

Marty Sklar, former vice chairman and principal creative executive at WDI, holds the distinction of being the only person who attended the opening day of every Disney park worldwide. Although his influence in WDI has been vast, Sklar reveals what he considers the true source of inspiration: "All of Walt Disney World is a reflection of Walt Disney's vision, leadership, and imagination, and especially confidence. Confidence and optimism of what the future can be." Sklar, now a Disney Legend, continues his involvement as an international ambassador for WDI.

A window worth noting belongs to Frank Wells, chief operating officer and president of Walt Disney Company from 1984 to 1994. Look for the window titled **Seven Summits Expeditions,** up on the third story, above the Main Street Market House. Wells's window is the highest on Main Street, in honor of his love for mountaineering. But consider this: Wells attempted to conquer the highest summit on each of the seven continents in a single year—achieving six of the seven, but having to turn back before reaching the top of Everest. Coincidentally, there are also seven (count 'em!) lands at Magic Kingdom and Mr. Wells conquered them all.

✱ Fascinating Fact

If anyone had been doing some investigation into who was mysteriously buying up vast acreages of land in central Florida, they would have found the chairman of each of the dummy companies was a certain Mr. M. Mouse! The whole secretive operation was given the codename Project X by Walt. It was finally brought to light by a reporter from the <u>Orlando Sentinel</u> who flew to Los Angeles to interview Walt and discovered he had an intimate knowledge of all the property taxes of the Orlando area. When the story broke, the cost of land in the surrounding area skyrocketed from $180 per acre to more than $1,000 per acre. The last few acres Walt purchased cost $80,000 each. ✳

You can find just about anything on Main Street U.S.A., including **singing and dancing lessons**. Turn right off Main Street, down the first street past Main Street Cinema. If you stand between the tables in the small café area near the Art Festival sign and the trellised balcony, you will hear voice lessons coming through an upper-level window across the street. Keep listening and you may also hear tap-dancing or piano lessons.

As you return to Main Street, the building on the corner holds another nostalgic bit of hidden magic. In Walt's boyhood, a trip to the General Store was as much a social event as an opportunity to put in a supply of necessities. When phones were just coming into common usage, most were on party lines, meaning many homes shared the same connection. Pick up the **wall-mounted telephone** in the General Store on Main Street, next to the cash register near the front. When you hold the receiver up to your ear, you will hear a conversation between the upstairs resident and her daughter. Stay on the line long enough and you will hear the nosy neighbor listening in and giving her thoughts on the discussion!

Your attention will probably be focused on the castle now that you are getting closer, but notice how all the **shop windows** along Main Street are lower than traditional architecture would place them. Walt wanted small children to be able to see inside, which would not have been possible had they been set at their correct height.

The warm, comforting smell of **home-baked cookies** follows you through town, until you reach the end of the street. On the left, Casey's Corner serves up hot dogs, the ultimate American picnic-and-baseball food. On the right you'll find Plaza Ice Cream Parlor, the turn-of-the-century setting for young love. You are right on the brink of Nineteenth Century U.S.A., with all the hopes and dreams of the American spirit backing you up and urging you onward!

Now you have reached the far end of Main Street, look at the upper window above The Plaza Restaurant, facing Cinderella Castle. There, you will find **Walter Elias Disney's window**, the director of the Show. His window reads: *Walter E. Disney. Graduate School of Design & Master Planning. "We Specialize in Imagineering."* While the director's name always comes first and last in the credits, the sentimental version of this placement dictates Walt has been given an eternal view of the castle.

Imagine That!

When asked what small details he enjoys most and wishes others would pause to see, Jim Hill, award-winning author, long-time Disney watcher, and webmaster of JimHillMedia.com, says, "I always got a kick out of sitting at Main Street up on the train station, and watching the five P.M. flag ceremony inside the parks. It's typically veterans or people associated with 9/11 who get to do this. They get to take part in the ceremony and afterwards they're presented with the flag they've taken down and they get the special pin. So many people these days are so under the gun to recover the money they spent on their vacation they don't take the time to appreciate the

details, the little storytelling that's going on that could really make
the entire trip. Tell people to put the brakes on."

Below Walt's name are the names of his **master planners**—Richard Irvine, John Hench, Edward Brummitt, Mar-
vin Davis, Fred Hope, Vic Greene, Bill Martin, and Chuck
Myall—who were primarily instrumental in designing the
Magic Kingdom.

Walt also has a **window on the front of the train station**,
directly above the Magic Kingdom sign, before you enter
the park. It is the only window you can see from outside the
park and it honors Walt's love of trains. It reads: *Walt Disney
World Railroad Office, Keeping Dreams on Track, Walter E. Disney, Chief Engineer*. Remember to look back as you're leaving
the park, to see this special remembrance.

Then, as you transition through the Hub area, step
beyond the embrace of Hometown America and enter Old
World Europe as represented by Fantasyland.

Fantasyland

Welcome to the quintessential Disney experience, the epit-
ome of all Walt dreamed of in family entertainment. Fantasyland brings the tales gathered by the Brothers Grimm to
life through the graceful charm of European castles, knights,
and ladies fair; it is the embodiment of childhood fantasy
that has been passed down from grandparent to grandchild
throughout the ages.

The Show element is fairly obvious: You have entered
the cinematic world of the Disney classics. A more history-
based storyline brings you out of Hometown America into

the charm and gallantry of medieval Europe. Billowing tents, heavy brick, and handblown glass windows evoke a feeling of long-ago kingdoms and quaint villages created through childhood imagination.

✳ Fascinating Fact

Each time you pass from one land to another, the landscaping, ambient sound, and architecture change subtly. For example, when transitioning from The Hub to Adventureland, the architecture and landscaping along the front of the Crystal Palace change from Victorian to more colonial style, the design elements on the bridge crossing into Adventureland become more primitive, and the landscaping takes on a more jungle-themed look. ✳

When you reach the far side of the central Hub (the area in front of Cinderella Castle from which the pathways leading to six of the park's seven lands originate) past the Partners statue of Walt and Mickey, turn around and notice how the pavement slopes gently upward from Town Square to Cinderella Castle. Fantasyland is actually on the "second floor," while beneath your feet, on the real "first floor," are the **Utilidors,** the tunnels, offices, and functional facilities of the park. Walt Disney World Imagineers could not dig a basement in Orlando as they did at Disneyland in California because the water table in Florida is too high.

The earth used to create the second floor came from what is now **Seven Seas Lagoon**, in front of the Magic Kingdom. The remainder of the Magic Kingdom is also raised, with the exception of Mickey's Toontown, which has no Utilidors below it. Why? Because it was the last land to be built and wasn't there when the park opened.

Those beautiful white-sand beaches in front of the Polynesian and Grand Floridian Resorts are natural to the area . . . sort of. After Bay Lake was drained and all the debris removed, white sand was found underneath. It was removed, cleaned of impurities, and used to form the beaches surrounding the Seven Seas Lagoon.

Standing at the end of Main Street looking at Cinderella Castle, the turrets appear much higher than their 189 feet. Imagineers used a technique called **forced perspective** to give the castle a towering presence while keeping the actual height under 200 feet, which would require it to have airplane beacons, thus ruining the illusion.

Imagine That!

Forced perspective is a technique used to trick your eye into thinking something is bigger, taller, closer, or farther away than it actually is. Imagineers use this technique throughout Walt Disney World to make the most economical use of space and materials. Many of the buildings you see are built, for example, to an 80/60/40 scale, meaning the lower level is built to 80 percent normal scale, the second level to 60 percent, and the upper level to 40 percent, giving the illusion of greater height.

The **Utilidors** also serve as a system through which Cast Members (the designation Walt Disney gave to all Disney employees to show that they were an integral part of the Show) move from one land to another without appearing in a land for which their costume is not appropriate. You will never see a Frontierland Cast Member in Tomorrowland, just as you will never see one land's theme when you are in another land. There is always some obstruction, either visual or auditory, to distract attention from any structure

Disney does not want guests to notice. Where an obstruction could not be created, the theme of whatever could be seen in another land was designed to blend with that land as well as the land it is in.

Cinderella Castle

Did you know it isn't called **Cinderella's Castle**? It's Cinderella Castle, without the possessive tense. Wholesome as it is, at one time the castle presented a moral dilemma when the restaurant inside was called King Stefan's Banquet Hall. There were raised eyebrows over Sleeping Beauty's dad having a room in Cinderella's castle; so, in 1997 the restaurant was renamed Cinderella's Royal Table.

As you approach Cinderella Castle, notice the **three-circled design** of the stone fence running along the walkway toward the entry to the castle, which, at the right time of day, casts Mickey's silhouette. Even more interesting is the fact the central rose had to be added after the fence was built because young guests kept sticking their heads through the openings and getting stuck! You can still see the original design if you look at the front of Cinderella Castle, to either side of the clock.

Before you enter the castle, look up. An **apartment suite** was included in the original design of the castle, although Walt passed away before it was built. His brother Roy was offered the suite, but declined. It became a storage location and is now used as an area for castle area performers to relax.

If you have a sharp eye, you may also see the **Disney family coat of arms** standing guard over the front and back entrances to the castle.

Inside the breezeway, on the left-hand side, is a **mosaic** telling Cinderella's story. Her wicked stepsisters Drizella and Anastasia show their true colors, with their faces crafted in green and red tiles, belying their evil emotions. One is "green with envy" and the other "red with rage," and in scenes where their eyes are open, they shine like jealous emeralds.

Glance at the columns along the walkway inside the castle, and you'll see each is carved with tiny **forest friends** from the Cinderella story, a beautiful example of attention to detail even when it isn't strictly necessary.

Every day around 3 P.M., guests who are not dining at Cinderella's Royal Table may enter the restaurant to look around. If you visit, notice **Jaq and Gus**, Cinderella's faithful friends, up in the rafters in the lobby.

The crests adorning the lobby walls and the banners inside the restaurant are the **family emblems** of various Disney executives and Imagineers. Ask a Cast Member if you can see the book that identifies each coat of arms.

Passing behind the castle you'll see a **fountain** with Cinderella's likeness off to the left. When you bend down to take a drink from the water fountain in front of her, you are symbolically bowing to the princess, whose crown now appears on her head. Children, however, never have to bow to the princess.

✴ Fascinating Fact

Contrary to one of the great urban myths, Marilyn Monroe was not the inspiration for the curvy character Tinker Bell in the 1953 Disney movie, Peter Pan. Margaret Kerry, actor, dancer, and voice talent, was the real reference model for the fairy, although she was not listed in the movie's credits. But there was more to it than that. Margaret explains that when creating the beguiling little pixie with animator Marc Davis and co-director Gerry Geronimi, she asked them,

"'Is there any way that you want me to play her? Do you want me to play her aloof? Is she funny, is she a clown? What is she?' Marc Davis told me, 'We like your personality. We just want you to be you.' So when you see Tinker Bell, that's exactly me. I could put in almost anything I wanted to for Tinker Bell to make her come alive." She adds, "The first thing they asked me to do was the famous scene where I land on the looking glass. I had made up my mind I would play Tinker Bell as if she were about 12 years old and the whole world was her oyster. She had never seen most things that she was about to see, and I figured that she had never seen a looking glass. Why should she? Why would they have that on Neverland? So I played it looking at myself, and although they put it down that she's a preening pixie, actually I played it as if she's saying, 'Oh, is that what I look like! Oh!' All except my hips. I was very unhappy with the size of my hips, so that's why Tinker Bell stomps off." ✳

Do you have a Tinker Bell fan in your group? Try to arrive thirty minutes before the posted opening time at Magic Kingdom so you are among the first to enter the park. When guests are allowed into the various lands at rope-drop, walk directly through Cinderella Castle into Fantasyland, to **Tinker Bell's Treasures** (on your left). The first person to enter will be allowed to "awaken Tinker Bell" by releasing her from the wooden box on a shelf behind the cashier's till, near the back of the shop.

If you are not among the first to visit, you can still see the **pixie dust trail** she leaves as she flies around the shop throughout the day. For a special view of the precocious pixie, take a look in the first **keyhole** in the sewing drawer next to the door at the front of the shop.

While you are in the shop, notice how it is divided visually into two separate themes, both from the *Peter Pan* story.

The section nearest Cinderella Castle represents the **Darling children's nursery**, while the section farthest from the castle represents **Captain Hook's ship**, with the ship's wheel serving as a transition between the two themes. Each section's décor is appropriate to its theme.

Pay a visit to **Sir Mickey's Shop**, just across the pavement from Tinker Bell's Treasures. The theme is based on Disney's adaptation of *Jack and the Beanstalk*, the last Disney short in which Walt himself voiced Mickey Mouse. If you look at the ceiling at the back center, you'll see **Willie the Giant** trying to lift the roof in search of Mickey.

Just before you reach Cinderella's Golden Carrousel, you will see the handle of **Excalibur** from the King Arthur legend, protruding from an anvil, waiting for the heir to the kingdom to remove it and take his (or her) rightful place on the throne. A lovely little show used to make its home here. At various times, the wizard Merlin would choose youngsters (in an elaborate ceremony) to try their hand at removing the sword.

Before you move on, look down at the pavement surrounding Excalibur. The bricks are shaped like the **blade of a sword**. It's one of those little "unnecessary" things that really pulls the whole theme together.

Next, look for **Cinderella's horse** on Cinderella's Golden Carrousel. It is the second horse in, with a golden ribbon around the bottom of its tail. Lovely, isn't it? The competition among all the little princesses who want to ride Cinderella's horse isn't quite as pretty, though!

To the left of the carousel is Mickey's PhilharMagic, one of the most creative attractions in the Magic Kingdom, with a charming secret that may go unnoticed by first-timers and veterans alike. With all the sensory input, you may miss a delightful extra—or you may wonder if you imagined it!—as the scent of **jasmine** and **apple pie** waft over you at various points during the show.

The only way to meet a mermaid is to go "under the sea," and the only place to meet Ariel is in **Ariel's Grotto**, toward the back of Fantasyland. As you approach the entrance, look down at the pavement. A sandy beach full of seashells transitions you from land to sea, then the squirt fountains take you underwater and into the current toward Ariel's home.

To the right of Ariel's Grotto is a small tribute to the long-gone but ever-popular 20,000 Leagues Under the Sea attraction, which used to be located where Pooh's Playful Spot now resides. Inside the play area's centerpiece tree, look for a **picture of a submarine** over the inside of the tree's front door, representing Captain Nemo's *Nautilus*.

The Many Adventures of Winnie the Pooh

This attraction debuted in its original form in Tokyo Disneyland as Pooh's Hunny Hunt, but the appeal is international. Children everywhere find it impossible to resist the cuddly cubby, in spite of the fact he and his forest friends took over the home that once belonged to the popular Mr. Toad.

When your ride vehicle enters Owl's house inside the attraction, turn around and look behind you. You will see a picture on the wall showing Mr. Toad from *Wind in the Willows* handing the **deed** to his house to Owl. Many WDW guests were unhappy to see Mr. Toad's Wild Ride make way for the Pooh attraction, so the Imagineers gave a nod to Toad's popularity and a subtle stamp of approval by having Toady give the deed to the new owner.

On the left of the floor in the same area, leaning against some other pictures, is a **painting of Pooh with Mole** from *Wind in the Willows*. Another nod of approval? You be the judge.

Imagine That!

Inspiration comes from many places, including the target audience. Imagineer Eddie Sotto recalls, "When I was involved in Tokyo Disneyland, we wanted to create a Winnie the Pooh attraction that would be beyond anything that had ever been done. The 'Hunny Pot' themed ride vehicles were wirelessly guided without tracks, allowing them to go backwards, spin, and roam freely through the show. It was stunning, but there was still something missing. How did that relate to the story we were trying to tell? We then surveyed little kids and asked them what they would most want to do in a Winnie the Pooh attraction. The answer we got, loud and clear, was to 'bounce in the forest with Tigger.' We then spent the next several years developing a magical effect that would allow each vehicle to actually 'bounce' with Tigger."

It's a Small World

Possibly the best-known attraction in Walt Disney World, It's a Small World has a simple, childlike style that is a real departure from the more traditional artistic renderings used by the Imagineers. Artist Mary Blair's unique style appealed greatly to Walt Disney, as it does to young children who, in spite of the all-too-catchy tune, insist on ride after ride.

Although Imagineer Mary Blair chose white to represent the world community because she felt it was festive, it's interesting to note that when red, blue, and green (the three primary colors in light) overlap, the resulting color is white. Want to see more of Mary Blair's work? Check out the 90-foot-high mural inside Disney's Contemporary Resort.

As you wander Fantasyland, you may notice many attractions are housed under tent facades, giving the land the feel of a medieval fair. Although it is a bit difficult to make the mental connection between Small World and a medieval festival, it's obvious the columns out front are carved into the shape of **jousting lances**. Why did the Imagineers choose a **medieval fair theme** for Fantasyland? They didn't, really. Many of the Fantasyland attraction facades were not quite finished when Disneyland opened in California in 1955, so banners and decorative tents were used to cover the unfinished parts on opening day, and the theme stuck!

Cross the walkway from Small World for a journey to Neverland in the Peter Pan's Flight attraction, and remember to look around before your ship flies out the nursery window. Watch for the **building blocks** near Wendy's bed and just under the window, which spell out P Pan and Disney.

And now, exit the attraction and pass under the **transition area** to your left; this moves you from Fantasyland into Liberty Square. Each time you pass from one land to another, the sights and sounds change subtly. In keeping with the theme of the Show, you are now undergoing a scene change. The transition area is darker, symbolic of a fade-out, the music and ambient sound change, and when you emerge on the other side, you find yourself in Early America. Turn around and look at the backside of what was a Tudor home in Fantasyland. It has become the upper story of a colonial home.

Liberty Square

Passing into Liberty Square, you have entered the New World. The footbridge over the river between the central Hub area and Liberty Square symbolically takes you across the ocean to the East Coast of the United States, while the transition area near Peter Pan's Flight takes you from London into colonial America. It didn't take long for the colonists to begin their westward trek, and it won't take you long to cross into Frontierland, but there is much to discover in the New World if you take the time to look.

There are four eras represented in Liberty Square, with a **New England** feel surrounding the Columbia Harbour House restaurant, **colonial Williamsburg** near Ye Old Christmas Shoppe, and the more modern **Dutch New Amsterdam** as you near the footbridge to the Hub. The Haunted Mansion attraction is technically part of Liberty Square, representing **New York's Hudson River Valley**.

Imagine That!

What does it take to become a member of WDI? Imagineer Eric Jacobson, senior vice president of Creative, WDI, says his passion began in childhood. "One of my hobbies as I was growing up was model trains and miniatures, and especially creating miniature worlds. I really appreciated the attention to detail that went into the Disney attractions and shows, so I always thought it would be really fun to design rides and these imaginary worlds. I got a job in Disneyland as a performer in the entertainment division in parades, and one thing led to another. I was an art major and they needed help in the art department to design various things for the Bicentennial celebration in 1976, so they started using me on a part-time basis. I met some Imagineers who were working at Disneyland at the time, building an attraction, and they set me up with an interview at Imagineering. They were gearing up to build and design Epcot, so I was hired in the model shop making miniature worlds. I've been with Imagineering for about thirty-one years now."

Columbia Harbour House offers more than just good food. Maps, artifacts, and nautical knickknacks adorn the walls, both on the first and second floors. Look closely and you'll notice each section is dedicated to either a **ghost ship** or a **ship lost at sea**. And, if you look out of the front windows from the top floor, you'll notice it faces the Haunted Mansion. Coincidence? I think not!

Another interesting tidbit can be found on the wall to the left of the window that overlooks the Haunted Mansion. *National Geographic* magazine published a map of the **Ghost Fleet of the Outer Banks**, and a copy is framed here. It marks the location of all 500 ships lost along the U.S. coastline from Chesapeake Bay in Virginia to the Core Banks of North Carolina. On the wall directly opposite, you'll see the name of this particular room. Fans of shipwreck lore (or of the *Pirates of the Caribbean* movies) will know the *Flying Dutchman* to be a phantom ship that wreaked havoc on the seas, striking fear into the hearts of sailors as a foretelling of doom.

Another tenuous tie that helps bring the Haunted Mansion into the theme of Liberty Square can be found in the restaurant's artifacts if you look at the beams above the area where you order your meal. See the fishing spears hanging on some of them? When you visit the Haunted Mansion, look for the same spear in the hands of the sea captain, whose portrait you will pass after you exit the stretch room.

Stroll around Liberty Square taking note of the doors, which all have a **two-digit number** on them. They are designed to look like a street address, but if you put "18" in front of the number, you have the year that style of house would have been popular. The date over the entry door to the Hall of Presidents is the year the United States Constitution was ratified.

As you observe the house numbers, also notice the slightly skewed angle of the **window shutters**. During the Revolutionary War, colonists had to use every scrap of available metal for making bullets; their ingenuity led them to recycle the metal hinges on imported shutters, replacing them with leather hinges, as was the tradition during pioneer days. With time and weather, the leather hinges became less taut, and the shutters slumped sideways.

In keeping with Walt's desire for authenticity, there are no restrooms in Liberty Square, except for those required inside the full-service restaurants, just as there would have been no **indoor toilets** during colonial times. But with their strict attention to detail, the park's designers placed the restrooms on the extreme left side of Columbia Harbour House, as that portion of the restaurant is geographically still in Fantasyland, and therefore in Europe, not in the New World.

Notice what looks like a river of **brown gravel** running through the pavement in Liberty Square? It represents an open sewer, where waste would have collected in the middle of the road, having been thrown from the upper windows of the homes. Now you know one reason ladies always carried a parasol!

Though it is often overlooked as just another part of the landscaping, Liberty Square Tree, the centerpiece in this area, has **thirteen lanterns** hanging from its branches; each lantern represents one of the original thirteen colonies.

✳ **Fascinating Fact**

While you're enjoying Liberty Square, take out a U.S. dollar bill and look at it. It has thirteen bars on the shield in front of the eagle, thirteen stars above the eagle, thirteen arrows in the eagle's talons, thirteen leaves and fruits on the olive branch, thirteen letters in both E Pluribus Unum (the banner held in the eagle's mouth) and in Annuit Coeptis (above the pyramid), and thirteen steps on the pyramid. It certainly isn't an unlucky number for the United States. Instead, it's a reference to the nation's proud beginnings. ✳

Ye Olde Christmas Shoppe, just to the right of Liberty Square Tree, represents the cooperative effort of three colonial families. As you enter, you are in a **German immigrant's** shop, the middle section is owned by a **woodcarver**, and the back section belongs to a **musician**. The scent of pine and cinnamon enhances a comforting sense of Christmas, family, and home, themes important to immigrants far from their loved ones.

Now look at the upper window of the home next to the door with number 26 on the front. See the lanterns up there? They represent the **two lanterns** hung in Boston's Christ Church steeple in April 1776, to warn Paul Revere the British soldiers were arriving by sea.

Walk around the corner of the same building and look at the upper window on that side. The country folk may not be up, but they certainly are armed! During the Revolutionary War, the townsmen would place their **rifle in the window** to indicate they were home and ready to answer the call to arms.

As you take in the Hall of Presidents attraction, you may wonder why there are only **forty-three animatronics** in the show given the fact that Barack Obama is the forty-fourth president. Grover Cleveland served as president twice, but in separate terms (he was the twenty-second and twenty-fourth president).

The Haunted Mansion

The Haunted Mansion houses 999 ghosts and nearly as many hidden secrets. The first greets you ominously, even before you set foot on the property. As you pass through the gates, look at the center section. Your first indication all is not right in this creepy country manor is the outline of a **batlike creature**, placed within the ironwork for all eternity.

Imagine That!

Occasionally the classic attractions undergo refurbishment, often to the initial dismay of Disney purists. But the sense of responsibility to the attraction's original ideals and to the guests who appreciate its comfortable familiarity is not lost on the redesign planners. Bob Zalk, Walt Disney Imagineer and Show producer, describes the sentiment: "The idea of going back into an iconic attraction and adding, changing, adjusting, removing elements—the standards are extremely high when you reach the finish line. We have to deliver. Unlike new attractions, re-imagining an established attraction carries with it its own sense of history and tradition that the entire team has to take into account. It's a big challenge, but an exciting one!"

The mansion itself is a fascinating structure, steeped in murder, mystery, and just a bit of whimsy, right to the rooftop. Do the ornamental stone pieces along the roofline look oddly familiar to you? Upon closer inspection, you'll notice they look a lot like **rooks, pawns, kings, and queens**. Claude Coats, creator of the Haunted Mansion's architecture, was said to be a true chess buff, so perhaps he put his signature on the roof. Disney officially insists those are not chess pieces, but now you have seen them, so you be the judge!

Ask a Haunted Mansion Cast Member to tell you the story of **Madame Leota's ring** and you will either get a detailed rendition or a stony look and a curt, "There is no such ring." After a 2007 refurbishment of the Haunted Mansion, the latter statement became the correct answer (sort of).

The bridal ring story had many variations, all of which revolved around Master Gracey, the owner of Gracey Manor (the proper name of the Haunted Mansion) and his forlorn bride, Leota, whose likeness can be seen throughout your journey. Look for her in the crystal ball, in the attic wearing her wedding dress, and at the end of the attraction as she bids you farewell. Master Gracey can be seen hanging by his neck from the ceiling rafters in the stretch room when the lights go out and, since a 2007 update, in various photographs in the attic.

There were many versions of how Leota died and how her wedding ring became imbedded in the cement outside the exit of the Haunted Mansion, but the Fact is, the ring wasn't a ring at all, it was the trimmed-off end of a metal post that was once used in that area and could not be completely removed. The small metal bit that looked like the diamond was the tip of a tool that broke off when a maintenance crew member tried to pry the remnants of the post out of the ground.

The one really strange fact here is that, despite what any Cast Member may tell you (and some have developed some really elaborate fables), originally there was no backstory to the Haunted Mansion, either. For all its wonderful creativity, the Imagineers never developed a full theme around Master Gracey and Madame Leota, so we were left to our own imaginations as to what really happened to the tragic, ghostly bride.

As you are walking through the canopied part of the line, notice the eerie shape of the **pillars** on either side of the front door. Perhaps they are the two coffins left there for future occupants, which is pretty creepy!

The mansion itself is always a little bit spooky, but even more so at night. Once the sun goes down, cast an eye toward the top-story window above the front door. If you look up at just the right moment, you'll see what appears to be a **ghostly figure** passing by.

Remember Big Top Theatrical Productions on the upper-story window on Main Street? Imagineers Marc Davis and Claude Coats, who were instrumental in creating the Haunted Mansion, are honored in Gracey Manor's graveyard, just before you enter the mansion. Look for the tombstones for Brother Claude and Grandpa Marc. Imagineer Tony Baxter of **The Camelot Corp.** rests in peace as Brother Dave, and **Lake Buena Vista Magic Lantern Slides'** Imagineer Yale Gracey, who created many of the special effects that make the Haunted Mansion a true Disney Classic, is the infamous Master Gracey.

Other names found on Main Street are also honored on the mansion's tombstones. In particular, the tombstone for **Francis Xavier** honors Imagineer F. X. Atencio, who also wrote the words for "Grim Grinning Ghosts" (the *Haunted Mansion*'s theme song), "Yo-Ho" (A Pirate's Life for Me) from *Pirates of the Caribbean*, and the epitaphs on the tombstones. And, while you are enjoying Pirates of the Caribbean, listen for the voice saying, "Dead men tell no tales." Yup, that's F. X. Atencio's voice!

Madame Leota has the most dramatic headstone in the graveyard. Just before you go through the front door, look at the large tombstone to your left, where Leota's beautiful face is carved into her headstone. But wait, because while you're busy looking at her likeness, she may just wake up and look at you!

✳ Fascinating Fact

Madame Leota was, in reality, Leota Toombs, who worked in the modeling department at Disneyland California. Walt once told her she had the perfect face for the Haunted Mansion, but he meant it as a compliment. Ms. Toombs was a beautiful woman. It is her face you see in the floating Crystal Ball, but her voice was dubbed by Eleanor Audley, who also voiced Maleficent in Sleeping Beauty. ✳

Once you have entered the Haunted Mansion, you will be directed to stand in the dead center of the stretch room, which takes you to the waiting area for the ride after a delightfully frightening pre-show. When the doors open again, everyone will move quickly out, allowing you time to stop for a moment and listen. You may just hear the **gargoyles** talking! If you listen closely, you can briefly hear them say, "Stay together" against a background of other obscure mumblings. Keep listening and you will also hear the stretch room stretching.

When you exit, look at the **moldings around the doors** in the waiting area and throughout the Haunted Mansion. The top corner moldings are in the shape of stylized skulls. How spooky!

You may recall one of the tenuous ties to Columbia Harbor House is the spear in the hands of the Haunted Mansion's **mariner**. Just before you enter the queue, look to your left. He's in the third picture down from the stretch room. Prior to the 2007 makeover, his portrait and ten others—collectively called the Sinister Eleven—occupied the first corridor in the Haunted Mansion, and their spooky eyes followed riders as they passed by.

When you enter your Doom Buggy, you are greeted by your **Ghost Host**. His voice sounds vaguely familiar, doesn't it? While it is easy to mistake his deep tones for another well-known actor's (Orson Wells), this one actually belongs to voice actor Paul Frees. Frees has a vast resume, including having voiced Ludwig Von Drake, Boris Badenov (from the *Rocky and Bullwinkle* cartoon series) and yes, even the Pillsbury Doughboy!

Orlando's weather can be quite quirky, but the weather around the mansion is even quirkier. As you travel from room to room, watch the **storm** through each of the windows. If you were paying attention in the stretch room, you will recall the massive clap of thunder and the lightning strikes, indicating a storm was raging outside. As you pass through the first room, lightning can be seen, but no thunder is heard. In the music room, you will hear thunder, indicating the storm is ongoing, but there is no lightning. However, in the room with the coffin, there are no storm elements at all. Once you reach the ballroom, thunder and flashes of lightning return, but by the time you enter the graveyard, the night sky is clear and bright. That's some wild weather!

Something is definitely odd about the hands on the **13-hour clock**, just past the corridor of doors, too. Are they gnarled twigs? If you look closer, you'll see those aren't twigs, they're **fingers**! Notice the fingernails? And, if you have a sharp eye, you'll see the shadow of a ghostly hand passing over the face of the clock.

Although you cannot read it from your ride on the Doom Buggy, the **sheet music** on the floor of the piano room reads *Et cum spirituo* (meaning, "And with your spirit"), and the composer's vocal instruction, "*bol n muen ne,*" is scattered across the left-hand page. The right-hand sheet has no words, only staff lines. Has the unfinished work doomed its composer to play for all eternity? If you look at the floor quickly as you pass by the piano, you can see a **shadow of the composer** as he plays.

A replica of the **pipe organ** used in filming the movie *20,000 Leagues Under the Sea* also makes its home here in the ballroom scene. The movie's original prop found a second life in Disneyland's Haunted Mansion.

✳ Fascinating Fact

How do the ghosts in the ballroom scene appear and disappear? The special effect responsible for their transparency is an illusion called Pepper's Ghost. In the mid-1800s, John Henry Pepper, a professor of chemistry at the London Polytechnic Institute, discovered a way to create the illusion using two very simple props. I won't give the magic away, but I will give you a hint: As you drive back from the park tonight, turn on the overhead light in your car for a moment and look at your windshield. I'll let you work it out from there (and no, one of the props is not a mirror)! Can't stand not knowing? Do an Internet search on Pepper's Ghost when you get back home. ✳

As you enter the graveyard section of the ride, notice not only the worried look on the face of the **caretaker**, but also the direction of his gaze. He isn't afraid of something he sees beyond you, he's looking directly *at* you! You have symbolically become the 1,000th ghost.

The **caretaker's dog** isn't looking well either, though he does look familiar. It is said Walt had a dog he was particularly fond of and his memory lives on in Rover, who makes an appearance here in the graveyard, in Carousel of Progress, and dangling the prison keys at the end of Pirates of the Caribbean.

As you pass by the **singing statues**, one voice may catch your attention, and perhaps make you hanker for a bowl of cereal. Why? Because that deep, melodic baritone belongs to Thurl Ravenscroft, the voice of Kellogg's Frosted Flakes mascot, Tony the Tiger. If it just makes you grouchy, blame it on another Ravenscroft credit: he also sang "You're a Mean One, Mr. Grinch" in the seasonal television favorite, *How the Grinch Stole Christmas.*

When you reach the end of the graveyard scene, you can't help but notice the singing **Viking woman**. Can you guess why she was placed in that particular spot? Because "it's not over until the fat lady sings!" Now she has sung and your ride is almost over.

The real Madame Leota, Leota Toombs, *can* be heard in the Haunted Mansion attraction. Although Walt felt her voice was too high-pitched and childlike for the spooky sound he desired for the crystal ball, her voice is heard right at the end of your ride. A **mini Leota figure** above the final door before you exit your Doom Buggy urges you to "hurry back! Hurry back!"

But there are two more secrets before you depart the grounds. As you exit, look to your left. Those **crypts** have names carved into them. Bid a fond farewell to Asher T.

Ashes, Hap A. Rition, Clair Voince, and others. Farther along, you'll find the dearly departed Faithful Friends in the **pet cemetery**.

The demise of Mr. Toad's Wild Ride, a Fantasyland classic, is honored in the pet cemetery. Look toward the far-left corner in the back of the cemetery and you will see a statue of **Mr. Toad** from *Wind in the Willows*. Although Mr. Toad's Wild Ride was popular with parkgoers, Toady himself was a rather despicable character. Among his accomplishments were reckless driving, resisting arrest, various hit-and-runs, cross-dressing, theft, and a jail break. Spoiled, rich, and self-serving, Toad still managed to work his way into visitors' hearts and remains a beloved character to this day.

Finally, in keeping with the lesson in U.S. geography, once you leave Liberty Square (the East Coast), you symbolically travel with the pioneers as they make their way westward into unknown territory and you make your way into a new land.

Frontierland

As you pass into Frontierland from Liberty Square, you are symbolically crossing the Mississippi River and journeying west. The transition is gentle but obvious. Building materials in Frontierland are rough-hewn. There is a sense of excitement in the air, as if a gunfight could break out at any moment. It's the land of Davy Crockett and Buffalo Bill Cody, where anything could happen!

Some people say the **metal plate embedded in the walkway between Liberty Square and Frontierland** by the Rivers of America symbolizes a bridge across the

Mississippi River, but there were no metal bridges during pioneer days, least of all over the Mississippi. This is a popular misconception, not something that Disney states. However, as more pioneers moved west, the bright glimmer of the Transcontinental Railway's train tracks eventually spanned the continent, linking both coasts.

Tom Sawyer Island

Located in the Rivers of America, Tom Sawyer Island is a great place for a midday break. But did you know the island also holds several secrets? As you explore, you may come across a **paintbrush** carelessly left by Tom as he rushed off to the swimmin' hole. If you turn the paintbrush in to an Island Cast Member, you'll be rewarded with (usually) a FastPass for a Frontierland attraction. You need to arrive first thing in the morning for the best chance at finding a brush.

Stroll down the pathway to the right of the boat dock to Harper's Mill. The gears that turn the water wheel hold an interesting little surprise for those who take the time to look. The large, horizontal gear in the middle is home to a little **bluebird** that has made her nest between the cogs. Fans of the *Silly Symphony* series may recognize the reference to the storm-tattered bluebird nest in the 1937 Academy Award–winning short *The Old Mill*, the first film to use the multiplane camera.

Imagine That!

Walt Disney's creative thinking extended well past theme parks and cartoon characters. He also invented the multiplane camera, which gave an illusion of depth to animated works. Using slides positioned in several layers, animation elements could be made to travel against a static background, spin in opposite directions or otherwise move at varying speeds, introducing a new level of dynamic creativity.

The **Ambush Cave** is a fun place for youngsters to burn off excess energy, and it holds a bit of a mystery among the geodes found in its depths. Notice how the water flowing at the base of the crystal wall seems to run uphill. It may take a moment to see, but that water is definitely flowing the wrong way. Mysterious? Maybe. Look more closely and you'll notice the floor is tilted to create an optical illusion for a bit of fun.

Pay a visit to Fort Langhorne, named for Samuel Langhorne Clemens, better known as Mark Twain, the author of *The Adventures of Tom Sawyer*, near the back of the island. There are **guns** in the turrets for a little impromptu target practice. You may even get a shot at the runaway train over at Big Thunder Mountain. If you happen to hit the train and you need to make a quick get-away, look for the **escape tunnel** at the bottom of one of the turrets!

Return to Frontierland and journey farther into the wilderness. As they pushed westward, the pioneers regularly encountered daunting obstacles, some of the four-legged variety, but you can be pretty sure the bears you encounter at the Country Bear Jamboree are friendly. Or are they? Look down at the floor when you enter the lobby. Are those **claw marks** . . . ?

Pecos Bill was the stuff of legend in the Old West, with stories told of his superhuman feats. He was "the toughest critter west of the Alamo," digging out the Rio Grande with a stick when he needed water and shooting out all the stars in the sky, save one, which became the symbol of the

Lone Star State, Texas. The **framed document** near one of The Pecos Bill Café and Tall Tale Inn and Café exits gives an abbreviated version of the Pecos Bill story. Look a little closer and you'll find Pecos Bill's **Code of the West**, offering menfolk some good advice about what not to do in front of women and children.

The Pecos Bill Café gives a nod to the Disney animated short story and, more important, serves as a transition out of Frontierland into the Mexican end of Adventureland. Take a look at the roof of the café. Notice how the front area is pure Wild West Saloon, but when you round the corner it takes a Spanish Mission–style turn, common in both California (represented by the Train Depot near Splash Mountain) and Mexico. It also blends harmoniously with the Caribbean theme as you move farther into Adventureland.

Having reached the West Coast and the train station at the terminus of the transcontinental railroad, you can't miss the two mountain ranges reaching skyward, but don't worry about them for now. Instead, head up the stairs to the train station itself, then stop and listen. You will hear Morse code emanating from the telegraph office, transmitting **Walt Disney's opening day speech** at Disneyland in California.

The train station's waiting room holds a rather unusual visual gag, on the shelf above the Lost and Found window. See that **wooden leg**? It could belong to Hopalong Cassidy, a famous American cowboy, in keeping with the western theme, but closer inspection reveals it has the name Smith scrawled across one side. Mary Poppins fans may remember Bert making the comment, "Speaking of names, I know a man with a wooden leg named Smith," to which Uncle Albert replies, "What's the name of his other leg?" Apparently the Brits made it to California along with the pioneers!

If you are ready for some time off your feet, take a round-trip journey on the Walt Disney World Railway. Imagineer Eddie Sotto tips us off to a bit of hidden magic here, in the form of the post-boarding announcement. He reveals, "I'm the conductor's voice on the WDW Railroad saying, 'Laaast Caaaallll Booooooard!'" and goes on to disclose that he is also heard "in some of the upstairs window voices and party lines on Main Street."

Splash Mountain

Splash Mountain (whose proper name is Chick-a-pin Hill) is based on *Song of the South* as told by Uncle Remus, but it has somehow made its home in the American West. Although technically it represents the Deep South (the states of Georgia, Florida, Alabama, Louisiana, and Mississippi) and should be painted deep clay-red to represent Georgia's soil, a little creative color mixing went into blending it more harmoniously with Big Thunder Mountain, thus maintaining the theme, at least visually.

Just as the pioneers had to make difficult decisions as they traveled west, guests, too, will have to decide if they're up for the final drop on Splash Mountain. Disney Imagineers thoughtfully placed a bridge at the foot of the mountain so guests could watch the logs as they plunge into the briar patch, but beware, hidden dangers lay in wait! Every third log creates a splash, insuring riders get soaked and so do those watching from the bridge. This feature isn't always working, but when it is, it can be either startling or refreshing, depending on the time of year.

Why don't all the logs splash viewers as the riders plummet down Chick-a-pin Hill? The splash isn't created by the logs. It is actually caused by a **water cannon** hidden in the landscaping!

As you are loading into your boat for a trip down Splash Mountain, notice the **flashing street lamp** in front of you. Clearly, it's flashing for a reason. While there could be some wonderful, hidden magic, it's really just an indication to the attraction attendants that the boats are about to go into motion. You may notice the same technique used on other attractions, including Toy Story Midway Mania! whose lights are hidden inside giant Tinkertoy wheels.

By the time you reach the final climb on Splash Mountain, you may not be paying attention to anything other than closing your eyes and holding on tight. But don't close them yet. Just as you begin your ascent, look up at the ceiling, where a little **gopher** pops his head out and shouts, "F.S.U!" It's another Imagineer signature at work, this time by a Florida State University fan.

Big Thunder Mountain Railroad

Big Thunder Mountain Railroad has become a true Disney classic, in part because it is a terrific coaster all the family can enjoy and in part because of its exceptional theme. Big Thunder Mine isn't a working mine anymore, having been tapped out during the gold rush. Now it's a ghost mine, but the old ore cars are still there, ready to take riders on a hair-raising journey.

Watch for the **miner** enjoying his bath as you zip around the track. He seems oblivious to the dangers that surround him, in the form of a couple of pesky skunks and a mountain goat with a taste for dynamite. But here's a challenge as you tour the park: There are three full-size bathtubs in the Magic Kingdom. One is here on Big Thunder Mountain. Can you find the other two? Give it a try, and then look at Solution 1 in Appendix B.

Never ones to pass up the chance for a little wordplay, the Imagineers have named each train on Big Thunder Mountain. Look for I. M. Brave, U. R. Courageous, I. B. Hearty, U. B. Bold, I. M. Fearless, and U. R. Daring.

Prior to 2002, guests with a sharp eye could see a **burning house** across the Rivers of America while whizzing around on Big Thunder Mountain. That house had been engulfed in flames for thirty-one years. Why? Because, as your guide says, it's made of firewood! Even sadder than that joke is the fact the house is no longer on fire. Pesky rules and regulations got in the way of a fun little gem that parkgoers had enjoyed for years.

✳ Fascinating Fact

Big Thunder Mountain Railroad can rightly claim the title of a Disney Classic, but did you know the California version is the first attraction created with no input from Walt? Although two attractions, Star Jets and If You Had Wings, debuted after Magic Kingdom's opening day and before Big Thunder, they were similar to Astro Jets and Adventure thru Inner Space at Disneyland, both of which opened in Walt's lifetime. ✳

A quick peek at the second-floor window of the saloon as your train roars past reveals a party in progress. It's the **"wildest party in the Wilderness,"** but you will see it only at night. During the day, the partygoers are probably sleeping it off!

Although mining did not begin in Utah's Monument Valley (the inspiration for Big Thunder Mountain's look) until the country was well established, there was definitely mining in progress here on the mountain. Look at the names on the crates as you wait in line. One of them belongs to **Lytum and Hyde Explosives Company**.

As you retrace your steps to the train station on your way into Adventureland, you have symbolically reached the West Coast, completing your cross-country trek. But lands beyond America are calling for those brave enough to face the dangers of the jungle, pirates on the high seas, and a room full of loud, singing birds.

Adventureland

With the comforts of Hometown America, the mellow charm of Europe, and the thrill of discovering the New World behind you, the next step is to head off on a grand adventure exploring Mexico, the Caribbean Islands, Polynesia, and oddly enough, the Middle East. In terms of the Show, it is the realm of *In Search of the Castaways*, *Jungle Book*, *Swiss Family Robinson*, *Aladdin*, and the *Pirates of the Caribbean* movie series.

As you round the corner from Frontierland into Adventureland, the architecture is distinctly Spanish. Moving farther along, the details transition beautifully into the flavors of a Caribbean island, both thematically and literally, and then become a whole new world as you fly over the imaginary Middle Eastern realm of Agrabah before you land, somehow, in the South Seas.

Pirates of the Caribbean

Pirates of the Caribbean recalls the 1700s West Indies during the time the Spanish were finding gold in what would become the United States. Before you entered the attraction prior to the 2006 update, which added Captain Jack Sparrow, you were greeted by iconic parrot **Pegleg Pete** perched above the doorway. Sadly, after the refurbishment, Pete was removed from the front entry and now sits next to the pirate whose leg hangs over the bridge near the end of the ride. His humorous greetings are silenced, but give him a nod and a wink when you see him anyway.

When you enter the turnstiles, get in the right-hand line. As you walk toward the boarding area, watch for a window with bars on it; it's on your right-hand side. If you look into the cell below, you'll see another Imagineer signature. Disney Legend Marc Davis has marked the attraction with his love of chess. The two **skeletons playing chess** are at a total impasse. In keeping with the Imagineer's obsession with accuracy, Davis researched past masters tournaments for a no-win outcome, and the chess pieces were correctly placed on the board between the skeletons so they would appear to ponder their next move for eternity.

In the same line, just before the turnstiles where you will board your boat for a swashbuckling trip around the Caribbean, look for a **tunnel** on your right-hand side. Listen closely and you will hear the pirates digging; if you wait just a moment, you might hear some of their conversation.

More of the magic continues once you board your boat. Just after you enter the auction scene, you'll hear a pirate on the left shoot his gun. If you turn to the right when you hear it strike its unintended target, you will see the result of his lousy shot. No matter how many times that sign has been hit, it's still in pretty good shape!

Remember our Haunted Mansion ghost host? Paul Frees lent his voice to this attraction as well, and to many of the marauders, including the **auctioneer.** See if you can identify his voice in some of the other pirates on your journey.

As your boat nears the end of the auction scene, look up at the pirate sitting on the bridge. He has **real hair** on his leg and dirt on the bottom of his feet. Because he is the only pirate your boat comes close enough to see in great detail, he was designed to be as realistic as possible.

Although it is difficult to see in the dark, look for the crest as you pass by the last scene, above where Jack Sparrow is laughing over his loot. Wouldn't you know it, Imagineer Marc Davis came as close to a signature as possible when he added the faintly Spanish-sounding name **Marco Daviso** to the crest. Mr. Davis didn't miss another chance to express his love of chess. He has placed **rooks** in the upper right and lower left corners of the crest.

Imagine That!

Imagineer Sue Bryan credits teamwork—and fun!—when exploring new show and attraction ideas: "There are a lot of different ways that we begin conceptualizing a new attraction. Sometimes the parks have a particular need operationally, or they have goals, and we move in whatever direction we need to in order to meet those goals. But we certainly are partnering with different groups to try to meet needs. And then we have pure Blue Sky, where it's just people in a room saying, 'Okay, what would be cool? What have people never done before? What things could change our business in new and exciting ways?' It's really a balance between those two."

As you exit your boat, look down at the moving walkway. Is it possible **peglegged Davy Jones** passed this way? Those footprints could only belong to him.

It was vital to make the most of the space available while maintaining the correct theme in each land. To that end, the Adventureland side of the walkway linking to Frontierland near Aladdin's Magic Carpets is Polynesian in style. If you walk through the passageway, however, and look at the same walkway from the Frontierland side, it looks like a horse-and-carriage entryway.

Having magically arrived in the Middle East, take a look at the ground surrounding Magic Carpets of Aladdin. The **jewels scattered underfoot** are fit for the feet of a prince, but as you walk past and admire them, watch out for the camels—they spit!

The Enchanted Tiki Room, an idea spawned by a small **mechanical bird** Walt purchased, was originally conceived as a dinner show. However, it became so complex and cumbersome, the dinner show portion was scrapped and the concept became the first Audio-Animatronics show in Disneyland California.

The Jungle Cruise

Anyone twenty-one or over who has spent some time in the Adventurer's Club at Disney's now defunct Pleasure Island might recognize some of the **names on the FastPass machines**, made to look like shipping crates, in front of Jungle Cruise. Look for a crate intended for delivery to Pamela Perkins, president of the Adventurer's Club, and if you know the Adventurer's Club members, see if you can find other names in the waiting area.

Check out the list of **missing boats** in the Jungle Cruise line. It seems some of their passengers (such as Ilene Dover) are missing, too. Perhaps that's the risk you take when you traverse the Amazon, Congo, Nile, and Mekong rivers all

in one go, and since you are about to do just that, you may
want to keep an eye on everyone in your group!

Just after you pass through the Jungle Cruise turnstiles,
notice there is a large, hairy, scary **tarantula** in a cage on your
right-hand side. Ask the attending Cast Member about the
spider. Go ahead . . . ask!

While you're waiting in line for the Jungle Cruise, look across
the river. See that **small hut** that looks like it has a straw roof?
With the heat, rain, and humidity in Florida, that roof wouldn't
last long if it were real straw. Instead, it's made of metal strips.
The ability to create a lasting thatched roof was only implemented once Disney's Animal Kingdom was under construction.
Authentic thatching grass and Zulu craftsmen were brought in
from KwaZulu-Natal in South Africa to create the thatched roofs
you see in the Africa section of Animal Kingdom.

As you travel the rivers, your boat will pass by the rear
half of a crashed **Lockheed airplane**. The front half can be
seen in the Casablanca scene at Disney's Hollywood Studios'
Great Movie Ride, which holds another surprising secret.

Nearing the end of your cruise, listen closely to the native
crouched in the bushes on the left-hand side. He very clearly
shares his passion for the 1970s by saying, "**I love disco!**"

Although it is true the **Polynesian Resort** is placed directly
across Bay Lake from Adventureland, in keeping with the
theme, it is not true (as popular belief would have it) that
you can only see it from Adventureland. You can, in fact, see
it from the train as you near the Main Street Station, just as
the train affords a view of the Contemporary Resort, which
was placed near the Tomorrowland side of the park. But why
quibble about something so small? It's still inspired thinking to have placed the resorts directly across from the land
they best represent.

Imagine That!

Jim Hill, a well-known Disney expert, speaks to the evolution of park-goers' expectations, when he says, "Think about how slowly Pirates of the Caribbean sets the scene. You make your way through the Spanish Fort, you go down the drops and you're in that environment. What people want today is a three- or four-minute long, intense experience, then they want to get in line for the next intense experience. That's why the Imagineers embrace the idea of putting Disney characters into things. You can start a story that much faster if you go, 'We're in Stitch's world right now and this is where he's incarcerated.' You get that concept very quickly. Consider the Enchanted Tiki Room. In the '60s, people were mesmerized by a show with singing birds. It was the most amazing thing they'd ever seen."

Tomorrowland

After exploring the world, the next frontier to conquer is the future, specifically as it relates to Space. The Show theme of Tomorrowland is firmly of the science-fiction variety, with all things metal and machinery, most of it in motion. Even the pavement puts you in mind of the planets and what's out there just beyond our reach. Things buzz around you and above you, with progress as the theme du jour.

Tomorrowland was intended to be a **working city** and the headquarters for the League of Planets. As you look around, notice all the community's needs are catered for: transportation, news, dining, shopping, and communication. Whether you're a human citizen, an alien, or a robot, everything you need is right here!

The first attraction you reach when you enter Tomorrowland from the hub is Stitch's Great Escape, housed in the building on your left. Many of the signs inside the attraction are written in a peculiar **alien alphabet**; however, they can be translated into English if you read carefully.

Over on the right, you'll find Buzz Lightyear's Space Ranger Spin. This is the attraction most likely to make children (and competitive men!) insist on a second or third ride so they can better their score. As you exit, take a look at the **mural** to your right, just across from the ride photo area, where you'll see Stitch in the lower left-hand corner, zooming around in this spaceship.

The **street lamps in Tomorrowland** appear much more high-tech than those in other lands. Look up at the lamp outside Tomorrowland Indy Speedway, and see if you can guess which famous mouse's shadow is cast on the pavement when the light shines just right.

Only Disney could make garbage fun! Keep an eye out for the motorized trash can that often hangs out around Mickey's Star Traders and Cosmic Ray's Starlight Café. Can you guess his name? It's **PUSH**!

News travels fast in the future. Take a look at the **Tomorrowland Times** being sold by the robot near Astro Orbiter, just to the right of the entry to Tomorrowland Transit Authority. Then, walk around to the right, toward The Lunching Pad fast-food counter. See the **phone booth**? By now, you know what to do. Pick up the receiver and listen!

✱ Fascinating Fact

There is a long-standing myth that claims the asteroids you see while zipping around Space Mountain are really pictures of chocolate chip cookies. Although it's an interesting thought, it isn't true. ✱

The Tomorrowland Transit Authority (formerly called the WEDway Peoplemover, after Walter Elias Disney) rarely has a line. It's a pleasant ride, especially when it's hot and you can truly appreciate the breeze. The TTA passes by a model of a city, giving us a glimpse of how Walt envisioned the **City of the Future** (which eventually came into being, to some degree, as Epcot), and it is the only place you can see inside Space Mountain from the outside.

Even more remarkable, though largely unnoticed by guests, is the fact the TTA travels its entire 4,574-foot length without the benefit of any onboard moving parts. It is all driven by magnets.

Listen closely as you near the end of your ride on the TTA. Hear that page for "**Tom Morrow, Mr. Tom Morrow**"? Tom was the head of Operations in the now-extinct Mission to Mars attraction.

Remember **Rover**, posing as the skinny hound in the graveyard scene inside Haunted Mansion? He makes several appearances in Carousel of Progress, which debuted at the New York World's Fair in 1964 and has been running almost continuously ever since. The dog has gone by the name of Buster, Queenie, and Sport, until finally he simply became Rover.

There is a slight, but forgivable, continuity error in the Carousel of Progress storyline, which spans approximately eighty to ninety years, beginning at the turn of the century and ending with virtual reality games and high-definition television. However, it's hard to ignore the fact the characters remain almost the same, appearing as if they have aged only a few years.

As you pass by Tomorrowland Indy Speedway heading toward the Mad Tea Party, stop and listen. Hear that sound? Nope, you don't, because there is no sound. You have entered the only area of the Magic Kingdom where music is not piped in. Why not? Because there was no natural way to link Tomorrowland to Fantasyland, so the Imagineers chose not to transition guests through music.

Having seen most of Earth and some of Space, the only place left to travel is the world of Imagination. It was the last land to be added to Magic Kingdom, but a natural fit in the house Mickey built. And that's exactly what you'll find there: Mickey's Country Home and the town his friends inhabit.

Mickey's Toontown Fair

You've traveled the physical world; now enter the world of Imagination! Toontown's brightly colored, cartoonish characteristics reflect the whimsical nature of its inhabitants, created so realistically that children (and children at heart) can't help but believe Mickey Mouse and his friends really do live and play here. Walt Disney's imagination brought them to life, and Mickey's Toontown Fair gave them a home. Adding to the atmosphere of believability, you can hear the sounds of crop dusting and farm animals waking for the day if you arrive in Toontown at first opening.

Need to use the restroom while you're visiting? Unfortunately, someone at Pete's Garage was a bit careless and dropped the **key inside the gas pump**. See it in there? But don't worry, you don't need a key for the real restrooms. They're located in the building just beyond the gas pump.

As you stroll around Toontown, you'll see plenty of evidence Mickey really is the Big Cheese. Even the **Toonhole** (manhole) **covers** feature his likeness.

Imagine That!

Voice actress June Foray could be considered an honorary citizen of Toontown, as she provided the voice when Grandma Duck debuted on This is Your Life, Donald Duck in 1960. Foray also was the voice of Lucifer the Cat in Cinderella and Grandmother Fa in the movie Mulan, but you may be more familiar with some of her other credits, such as Granny of Looney Tunes fame, Cindy Lou Who from How the Grinch Stole Christmas, and Natasha, Nell Fenwick, and Rocky the Squirrel from the Rocky and Bullwinkle Show.

The Barnstormer at Goofy's Wiseacre Farm

The Barnstormer is filled with visual gags—some obvious, some less obvious. If there is no line, you may be tempted to walk straight up to the loading area, but slow down a moment and enjoy the elaborate theme first. When you enter the barn, listen for the crop duster's engine. It's close and getting closer! Stand in front of the **chicken crates** just inside the entry to the ride and watch the chickens' reaction as the airplane buzzes by.

On the wall opposite the chickens, you'll see a Class Schedule for **Fido's Fearless Flight School**. Take a look at his humorous lecture offerings, such as "How to Land on All Fours."

The **glass lamp** inside the barn is a subtle joke, based on the industrial lighting term *jelly-jar lamp*. Here at Wiseacre, they take the term literally.

A more obvious visual joke is the **cutout of Goofy** on the barn wall. You had to know that was going to happen, didn't you?

Minnie's Country House

Just across the street from Goofy's Wiseacre Farm, Minnie has a country home. As you walk through her house, listen to her **answering machine**. Mickey and Goofy have both placed a call while she was out.

Minnie's talents extend to the artistic, and she spends some of her free time painting in the next room you enter. Look at her latest **artwork on the easel** in front of the window. At least now we know why Goofy crashed!

Head into the kitchen next, for a few fun surprises. If you look in the oven, you can see the **cake** she is baking, and it's definitely falling. Luckily, she has a backup for tonight's treat. Hear the **popcorn popping** in the microwave oven? If not, push the button.

After you exit Minnie's Country House, take a look at **Donald's Boat** just across the street. It is his boat not only because, well, it's his, but also because it is him! Notice how the colors exactly match Donald and his outfit, right down (or up) to his trademark cap? And to add that extra bit of personality, the boat is leaking madly, just as Donald does when he spouts off in his characteristic fits of rage.

Back on the other side of the street, County Bounty brings the fair to Toontown with an opportunity to meet all your favorite Classic Disney friends, and while every county fair gives out **first-place ribbons**, County Bounty holds a few surprising awards. Look for the winning entry of the Niftiest Knitting Award (Toby Turtle won) and the award for the Most Aerodynamic Cream Pie. Chip and Dale are the winners, but who was the unlucky victim of a face full of pie? Take a look at the imprint inside the pie and see if you can guess! (Hint: Stand way back for the best view. Give up? Find the answer in Solution 2 in Appendix B.)

There are few quiet locations in the hustle-bustle of the Magic Kingdom, but if you need some time away from the crowds, take a short stroll and enjoy the solitude along the **walkway** between Tomorrowland (to the left of Space Mountain's gift shop) and Mickey's Toontown Fair (to the right of the train station). Most guests never find this pathway, so it remains quiet all day.

Imagine That!

Imagineer Eddie Sotto shares his story of how Magic Kingdom provided the spark of imagination, and how "dreams really do come true."

"When I was a young boy I fancied myself as a 'Disneytologist,' dreaming of one day becoming an Imagineer. It was January 1971, our family was vacationing in Florida and through a friend of the family we were introduced to Don Edgren, the project director of Walt Disney World. Although he didn't know us and was over-his-head busy, Don graciously gave us a VIP tour of what was taking shape.

I still remember gazing at the raw steel and white fiberglass facades of Main Street through the rear window of his dusty Chevy Impala. We saw the whole park the way Walt saw it, in a state of becoming. To experience that at age twelve was extraordinary, never to be repeated. Or was it?

Fast-forward to March of 1986 and my first week at WDI as an Imagineer. Everyone was piling out early to attend the retirement of a Disney Legend. I decided to tag along and see if I could meet this guy. When I got there a man took the stage that looked familiar. It was Don Edgren! They asked if anyone had any stories about Don. To his shock, a much older twelve-year-old stepped up to the mike. It was a short story of inspiration and a man who didn't have time, but gave enough to inspire a young mind with a ride down Main Street, only to find that twenty years later that same kid would get hired as the show producer/designer for the next Main Street in Paris!

We had a great reunion, and years later, on that French construction site, I remember many happy times walking alone after the crews had gone, strolling through the steel framing of Main Street waiting for that familiar feeling to come over me. I was twelve again."

Although Magic Kingdom was not Walt Disney's primary intent for his great Florida Project (that honor goes to the next park we'll explore), in terms of the historical timeline it had to come first. Profits from the park were necessary to raise the funding needed for Walt's true pet project, EPCOT Center. But from the perspective of the Show, Magic Kingdom comes in second to none. Open your eyes wide as you tour and, I hope, imagine your own happy stories in this most magical of places!

Magic Kingdom Timeline

In 1958, the Disney Company hired a private consultancy, Economics Research Associates, to begin a quest to find the ideal location where Walt could build his second theme park. The study indicated the obscure sites of Ocala and Orlando in Florida were most suited to the project. By 1963, Roy O. Disney and attorney Robert Foster proposed the purchase of 5,000 to 10,000 acres of land, prompting Walt to pay a visit to the area and make a final decision. After viewing the options, he settled on Orlando as the location for what would eventually become Walt Disney World.

Acting under the name Robert Price, Foster purchased 12,400 acres at a mere $107–$145 per acre, later adding another 9,750 acres at a relatively low cost. The total land purchase would span nearly 30,000 acres at a final cost of a little more than $5 million.

The *Orlando Sentinel* originally agreed not to reveal Disney's involvement in the land purchases, but, by the end of May 1965, the cat was nearly out of the bag. In June 1965, the *Orlando Evening Star* ran a feature referencing forty-seven transactions by Florida Ranch Lands, Inc., a boutique brokerage firm that was eventually revealed as working on behalf of Walt Disney in securing central Florida property. On October 25, Florida Governor Haydon Burns confirmed Disney's purchase of the land and, on November 15, in the Cherry Plaza Hotel in Orlando, Walt, Roy, and Governor Burns formally announced plans to build the fledgling Disney resort.

Sadly, Walt never saw a single brick laid at the Florida location. He died of lung cancer on December 15, 1966. Roy O. Disney changed the name of the project from Disney World to Walt Disney World in honor of his brother, one of the great creative visionaries of the modern era. On May 30, 1967, ground broke for Magic Kingdom, The Most Magical Place on Earth.

Opening Day 1971

The Magic Kingdom's grand opening took place on October 1, 1971, to a crowd of ten thousand visitors and at a cost of $400 million. Attractions open that day were **Cinderella's Golden Carrousel, Country Bear Jamboree, Diamond Horseshoe Revue, Dumbo the Flying Elephant, Frontierland Shooting Gallery, Hall of Presidents, Haunted Mansion, It's a Small World, Jungle Cruise, the Mad Tea Party, Mickey Mouse Revue, Audio-Animatronics, Mike Fink Keel Boats, Mr. Toad's Wild Ride, Skyway to Tomorrowland** and **Skyway to Fantasyland, Snow White's Adventures, Swiss Family Treehouse, Tropical Serenade, Grand Prix Raceway,** and **the Walt Disney World Railroad.**

In addition, there were a full array of shops, dining options, a **Penny Arcade, House of Magic, Main Street Cinema**, various novelty vehicles, horse-drawn streetcars, and horseless carriages.

Admiral Joe Fowler **Riverboat** opened on October 2, with **Peter Pan's Flight** debuting the next day. On October 14, **20,000 Leagues Under the Sea** made its inaugural dive, and on Christmas Eve, the first guests blasted into outer space compliments of **Flight to the Moon.**

1971–1972: The Early Days

Admission into the park in 1971 was $3.50 for adults, $2.50 ages twelve to seventeen, and $1 ages three to eleven. Unlike today, guests then had a choice of two attraction tickets: an Adult 7-Attractions booklet ran $4.75. For an additional $1, adults could get an 11-Attractions booklet. Coupons allowed for one ride per coupon, from A-rides (such as Main Street Vehicles and Cinderella's Golden Carrousel) to E-rides (state-of-the-art attractions such as Haunted Mansion, Country Bear Jamboree, Jungle Cruise, and It's a Small World).

Roy O. Disney presided over Magic Kingdom's dedication ceremony on October 23, 1971. In November, the **Electrical Pageant** water parade made its first journey along Bay Lake while the Circle-Vision 360 film *America the Beautiful* debuted in Tomorrowland. December 1 saw the addition of a fourth locomotive, the *Roy O. Disney*.

Tragically, on December 20, Roy died of a cerebral hemorrhage. Control of Walt Disney world passed to Don Tatum, acting as chairman, with Esmond Cardon "Card" Walker serving as president.

Eastern Airlines, the official airline of Walt Disney World, sponsored the **If You Had Wings** attraction in Tomorrowland, which opened on June 5, 1972, featuring a cutting-edge Omnimover ride system. By October 1, Walt Disney World's first anniversary, 10.7 million guests had passed through its gates.

1973–1974: Something New

The year 1973 saw a barrage of new attractions, including *The Walt Disney Story* in April, **Tom Sawyer Island**, **Tom Sawyer Island Rafts**, **Plaza Swan Boats**, and the *Richard F. Irvine* **Riverboat** in May. But the most notable attraction debuted on December 15 when **Pirates of the Caribbean** opened in Adventureland. It would become a true Disney classic and go on to inspire a classic adventure movie series thirty years later.

America the Beautiful closed on March 15, 1974, reopening a day later with a new film, *Magic Carpet 'Round the World*, which lasted all of a year before being replaced by *America the Beautiful* again. **Star Jets**, the area's new centerpiece attraction, followed in November, providing a dizzying rocket-ride high above Tomorrowland.

By the end of 1974, Walt Disney World's popularity had grown to astonishing proportions. On December 29, a record 74,597 day-guests passed through the gates, causing the park to close due to capacity for the first time in its history.

1975: Liftoff for Tomorrowland

Long-awaited thrill-ride **Space Mountain** launched on January 15, 1975, adding a much-needed boost of adrenalin to an otherwise gentle park experience. Space travel remained very much in the public consciousness, though travel to the moon had lost some of its mystique. In response, Flight to the Moon became **Mission to Mars** on June 7, giving the attraction a new name and destination, although it remained essentially the same ride.

On June 6, **America on Parade** began running twice daily along Main Street's parade route in honor of the upcoming American Bicentennial.

A "great big beautiful tomorrow" arrived when the classic **Carousel of Progress** was moved from Disneyland in California to Magic Kingdom's Tomorrowland in 1975, with a new theme song, "The Best Time of Your Life." The original theme song would return in 1994, when the attraction was refurbished and renamed **Walt Disney's Carousel of Progress**.

1976–1981: Main Street Milestones

Although 1976 was quiet in terms of new attractions, the Magic Kingdom hit a milestone when day-guest Susan Brummer passed through the gates, achieving the distinction of being the park's fifty-millionth visitor.

Destined to be a Disney classic, **Main Street Electrical Parade** premiered on June 11, 1977. It would grace Magic

Kingdom twice, first for a fourteen-year run (1977–1991), and then again for two years (1999–2001).

The period from 1978 through mid-1980 was quiet at the Magic Kingdom as a second gate—EPCOT Center—broke ground in preparation for an October 1, 1982, opening. Mickey Mouse Revue closed at Magic Kingdom on September 14, 1980, followed by the retirement of the *Admiral Joe Fowler* riverboat. But big news came on November 8, with the opening of the park's second coaster, **Big Thunder Mountain Railroad**.

A Dream Called EPCOT film began showing at the EPCOT Preview Center in Magic Kingdom, generating excitement for the new park scheduled to open eleven years to the day after Magic Kingdom welcomed its first guests.

But 1981 also focused on Magic Kingdom's ten-year anniversary, with the stage show *Disney World Is Your World* and the **Tencennial Parade** running from October 1, 1981, through September 30, 1982, highlighting a celebration dubbed "a year long and a smile wide"—and smile wide, they did! Walt Disney World welcomed its 126 millionth guest during its Tencennial festivities.

1982–1983: The Quiet Years

Most of Walt Disney World's energy was focused on EPCOT through 1982 and 1983; hence, the Magic Kingdom had to endure several quieter years. The graceful Plaza Swan Boats no longer swam the park's inland waters as of August 1983, victims of ongoing maintenance problems. However, their main docking area, a green-roofed platform next to the rose garden between the castle and Tomorrowland, can still be enjoyed as a shady rest area today.

1984: A New Boss

A change in power occurred at Walt Disney World in 1984. Michael Eisner became the new chairman and chief executive officer following a major boardroom upheaval, with the company in the doldrums and losing money on both their theme park and film divisions. But the Magic Kingdom was not initially a primary focus for investment in new attractions.

A weak effort arrived in the form of the *Show Biz Is* show, which opened on July 12, 1984, only to close two months later. *America the Beautiful* was replaced by Circle-Vision film *American Journeys*, while the new **Frontierland Shootin' Arcade** offered little buckaroos the opportunity to spend a bit more of Mom and Dad's hard-earned cash on the chance to knock over a few prairie-themed targets. It was not a banner year.

1985–1987: More Development—But Not at Magic Kingdom

After the upheaval of 1984, it would take another four years before any new development occurred in Magic Kingdom. Time and money were focused on a rather quick decision to move forward with a third gate at Walt Disney World, the $300 million "Hollywood that never was and always will be" of Disney–MGM Studios.

In the meantime, **Merlin's Magic Shop** closed in Magic Kingdom in May 1986 and the Diamond Horseshoe Revue was renamed the **Diamond Horseshoe Jamboree**. Eastern Airlines was dropped as the If You Had Wings sponsor in January 1986, replaced by Delta Airlines. The name was changed to **If You Could Fly** on June 6. Capping off a rather uninspired year, *Magic Journeys*, the first in-park 3-D effort by Walt Disney Imagineering, debuted at the Fantasy Theater on December 15. The park would remain quiet throughout 1987, with no new attractions.

1988–1990: Junior Jamboree

The year 1988 would make up for the lack of investment in the park in the mid-1980s, especially for families with young children. **Mickey's Birthdayland** opened on June 18, originally intended to be a temporary Land for the duration of Mickey's birthday celebration.

The area consisted of **Mickey's House, Grandma Duck's Petting Farm, Mickey's Playground,** and three circus-style tents with character meet-and-greets and two live shows, including highlight show *Minnie's Surprise Birthday Party*. One of the prime attractions was a cow living at Grandma Duck's farm named Minnie Moo, born with the classic tri-circle Mickey head on her side.

Ending an ongoing struggle to find its identity, If You Could Fly closed for the last time on January 3, 1989. Debuting in its place, **Delta Dreamflight** opened on June 26 and became a guest favorite for its pop-up-book style and the illusion of entering a jet engine.

Due to its enormous popularity with families, the decision was made to keep Mickey's Birthdayland. It closed on April 22, 1990, reopening on May 26 under the name **Mickey's Starland**, with *Minnie's Surprise Birthday Party* replaced by the *Mickey's Magical TV World* show. Cheap cutout store fronts were replaced by more substantial facades.

1991–1993: Parades—and a Big Splash

September 14, 1991, saw the last running of the popular nighttime Main Street Electrical Parade. It was replaced on October 1 by the visually magnificent **SpectroMagic**. The

Surprise Celebration Parade ran each afternoon, beginning September 22.

It had been twelve years, though, since Magic Kingdom brought in a major attraction. Finally, in 1992, on July 17 (with a dedication ceremony on October 2), **Splash Mountain** generated screams of delight, with its gentle log flume ride through vignettes based on the1946 story *Song of the South* culminating in a final fifty-two-foot plunge with Brer Rabbit, straight into the briar patch!

The Walt Disney Story closed on October 5, 1992, followed by Mission to Mars on October 4, 1993. The Hall of Presidents underwent a major refurbishment, adding President Bill Clinton to the lineup on November 18, 1993, with new narration by poet Maya Angelou who had recited her poem "On the Pulse of Morning" at President Clinton's January 20 inauguration.

Also in November, the Carousel of Progress reclaimed its original theme song, "There's a Great Big Beautiful Tomorrow." On December 1, *Magic Journeys* at the Fantasyland Theater was presented for the last time. A month later, *American Journeys* closed, followed by Surprise Celebration Parade and Star Jets.

1994: The City of the Future

By 1994, Tomorrowland needed, and got, a major overhaul. It had begun to look dated, so in an effort to avoid that happening in the future, the Imagineers gave it a more general design, creating a "city of the future," with all the services of a major interplanetary metropolis.

In the process, the WEDway PeopleMover adopted the name, **Tomorrowland Transit Authority**, creating instant confusion for new visitors looking for the TTC (Transportation and Ticket Center). Despite the name change, many purists persisted in calling it the WEDway. Even more distressing, the classic attraction 20,000 Leagues Under the Sea closed, another victim of difficult maintenance.

1994–1995: Drama And Comedy

On July 8, 1994, *The Legend of the Lion King* show debuted in the former Mickey Mouse Revue theater, with a unique blend of animation from *The Lion King* movie, human-animal puppet performances, and some wonderful lighting effects. On November 21, 1994, **The Timekeeper** attraction with Circle-Vision film *From Time to Time* opened in Tomorrowland's Transportarium, with voices by comic duo Robin Williams as the Timekeeper and Rhea Perlman as time-traveling camera droid 9-Eye.

The wonderfully hometown Penny Arcade and the House of Magic closed on March 19, 1995, and on April 7, the Diamond Horseshoe Jamboree returned to its original name, the Diamond Horseshoe Revue. On the heels of the major refurbishment of Tomorrowland, Star Jets was reborn as **Astro Orbiter**, with the central rocket tower being replaced by a futuristic orbiting planets theme.

Flying in circles around Tomorrowland wasn't enough to hold teenagers' attention, so on June 20, 1995, the **ExtraTER-RORestrial Alien Encounter** began scaring the daylights out of little Mousketeers (and big ones). Incredibly innovative, Alien Encounter was the theme-park equivalent of a psychological thriller and ultimately proved too un-Disneylike, especially as a Magic Kingdom attraction.

1996–1997: Goofy for More

Mickey's Starland, now called **Mickey's Toontown Fair**, enjoyed an expansion in June, 1996, adding kiddie coaster **The Barnstormer at Goofy's Wiseacre Farm** (which replaced Grandma Duck's Petting Farm) and **Toontown Hall of Fame**. The Grand Prix Raceway's track was shortened to make room for the added attractions in Toontown, reopening on September 28 as **Tomorrowland Speedway**. On the other side of the park, the *Richard F. Irvine* riverboat was re-christened the *Liberty Belle*.

One of Disney's Nine Old Men, animator and railroad enthusiast **Ward Kimball**, received the honor of a namesake fifth locomotive, which made its debut at Magic Kingdom on March 1, 1997. That April, popular King Stefan's Banquet Hall restaurant was renamed **Cinderella's Royal Table**.

1998–1999: Silver Anniversary Stunner

After a May 17, 1997, accident dumped a boatload of guests into the Rivers of America at Disneyland California, the Mike Fink Keel Boats attraction there and in Orlando closed for good. Some Disney purists believed a more startling catastrophe occurred when Cinderella Castle was transformed into the **Cinderella Castle Cake** during Walt Disney World's *25th Anniversary Celebration* in late 1996, and they were delighted to see the balloon-like covering removed in January 1998.

On the strength of three enormously popular movies, *Aladdin, The Lion King,* and *Toy Story,* the Tiki Room reopened as **The Enchanted Tiki Room—Under New Management**, with Jafar's (from *Aladdin*) screeching parrot Iago acting as joint host with *The Lion King's* Zazu, while the brand-new **Buzz Lightyear's Space Ranger Spin** became an instant E-ticket hit.

Sadly, September 7 saw the closing of a Disney classic, Mr. Toad's Wild Ride. Toady handed over the deed to his former home on June 5, 1999, when the **Many Adventures of Winnie the Pooh** arrived.

2000–2002: New Millennium, New Shows

The year 2001 added new entertainment to the park, hot on the heels of a major promotion for Walt Disney World's *Millennium Celebration* in 2000. These included *Cinderella's Surprise Celebration* stage show, the daily **Share a Dream Come True Parade**, and the return of the nighttime **Spectro-Magic** parade, which replaced Main Street Electrical Parade on April 2. Geared toward the Dumbo the Flying Elephant crowd, **The Magic Carpets of Aladdin** provided a much-needed kiddie ride in Adventureland. On October 1, Disney's *100 Years of Magic Celebration* began, honoring the anniversary of Walt Disney's birth.

2003–2004: More Mickey and Friends

The 3-D multisensory treat *Mickey's PhilharMagic* took over the former Legend of the Lion King theater in 2003, a year after it closed. Nearby, the Diamond Horseshoe Revue closed, replaced by the ill-conceived **Goofy's Country Dancin' Jamboree**, a preschool free-for-all with Cowboy Goofy and Friends.

The poignantly beautiful **Wishes: A Magical Gathering of Disney Dreams** fireworks show lit up the sky for the first time on October 8, 2003, and four days later, The ExtraTERRO-Restrial Alien Encounter closed, a victim, perhaps, of its own success. The attraction set out to be terrifying—and did so in grand style.

Its replacement arrived on November 16, 2004, when the mischievous alien from the mega-hit move *Lilo and Stitch* teleported to Magic Kingdom with his own show, **Stitch's Great Escape.** Preschoolers were frightened by it, elementary-age kids loved it, and many parents dubbed it "just plain gross."

2005–2007: Movie Makeovers

New attractions were not high on the list for 2005–2006, but Disney could not ignore a generational problem caused by the wild success of 2003's blockbuster movie *Pirates of the Caribbean: Curse of the Black Pearl.* Youngsters clamored for the movie's star, played by the iconic Johnny Depp, prompting Audio-Animatronics of the inimitable Captain Jack Sparrow to be added to the Adventureland attraction.

In keeping with the trend of creating movie-inspired attractions, **The Laugh Floor Comedy Club** soft-opened briefly in December 2006, with one-eyed comedian Mike Wazowski of *Monsters, Inc.* movie fame acting as the show's Monster of Ceremonies. In December 2006 it was renamed **Monsters Inc. Laugh Floor Comedy Club**, finally settling on **Monsters, Inc. Laugh Floor** in March 2007. The attraction did not generate the screams of laughter expected, though many guests found the show's acronym to be hilarious, as it was, unfortunately, also an obscene pop-culture cinematic reference.

Urban legend came full circle during a major Haunted Mansion overhaul in 2007, formally introducing the ghostly bride storyline, which was not intended in the original design. Purists railed at the idea this classic attraction would be tampered with, but just as the Imagineers did a beautiful job in making Pirates of the Caribbean a more contemporary story without losing any of its original charm, so too did the Haunted Mansion's remake find favor. Some would argue it's better than ever!

Epcot

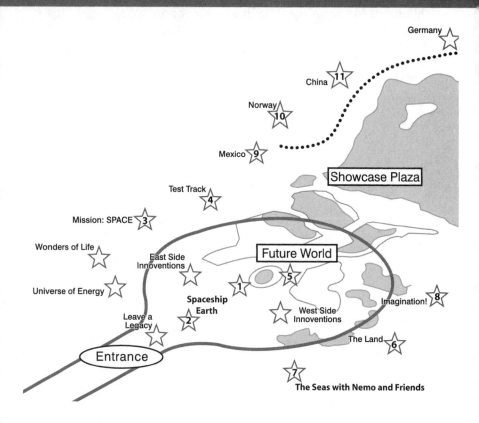

1. **Fountain of Nations:** The Innoventions Plaza's Fountain of Nations contains water from rivers and bodies of water around the world.

2. **Spaceship Earth:** This attraction was designed with a runoff system that prevents water from reaching the ground when it rains. Each panel funnels water away from the surface, eventually emptying into the World Showcase lagoon.

3. **Mission: SPACE:** The video monitors showing guests enjoying the ride actually display taped versions of the guest experience.

4. **Test Track:** When you enter the heat chamber, look left. Someone is making breakfast, with two eggs frying on a bit of aluminum foil on the heat compressor.

5. **Innoventions Plaza:** Aggressive birds used to frequent the outdoor dining locations. Why are they less pervasive at Epcot now? It is said the speaker systems play sounds of birds in distress, which keep hungry winged pests at bay.

6. **The Land:** As you watch the pre-flight video on Soarin', notice the flight number. It is 5505, honoring Soarin's official opening at Epcot on May 5, 2005.

Epcot

Italy
The American Adventure
12
Japan
Parade Route
Morocco
13
World Showcase
IllumiNations
World Showcase Lagoon
France
United Kingdom
International Gateway
14
Canada
World Showplace Events Pavilion

7. The Seas with Nemo and Friends: As you walk through the queue toward your Clam-mobile, notice the beach signs on the tall white signpost. If you look carefully at the advertisement for Daily Diving Departures, you will notice they are provided by Nautical Exploration & Marine Observation, or N.E.M.O.

8. Imagination: As you move into the upside-down room during your ride, notice the red and yellow paint pots. They're Figment Pigments, after the attraction's mischievous mascot.

9. Mexico: Why is it always twilight inside Mexico's Plaza de los Amigos? Because twilight is the time friends and family—relationships central to Mexican culture—gather in the plaza for socializing.

10. Norway: Look for the hidden Mickey in the giant mural in the loading area for the Maelstrom ride.

11. China: Look at the floor as you walk through the front doors of the Beijing Temple. Stand with your feet directly over the center circle in the group of concentric circles and say something, anything. The building is acoustically perfect, causing your voice to vibrate directly back into your ears.

12. The American Adventure: Surprisingly, Magic Kingdom isn't the only park with underground utilidors. As you walk toward the pavilion, notice how the land slopes upward. The attraction is actually on the second floor.

13. Morocco: Because Muslims believe no one is perfect but Allah, there are intentional design flaws throughout the pavilion.

14. Canada: To give the illusion of snowcapped mountains during the winter months, the Canada Pavilion's landscaping is replaced by all-white flowers and plants.

Chapter 2

Epcot

After the world journey of Magic Kingdom, Walt Disney World's second park comes as a complete change, focusing on the human journey toward invention, inspiration, and cooperation.

Epcot, the **Experimental Prototype Community of Tomorrow**, is a celebration of life, diversity, and the possibilities held by countless tomorrows. It is first and foremost a park dedicated to discovery; the unfolding of the natural world around us, anticipation of a world bettered by technology, revelations of humankind's differences, and more important, our similarities.

Walt Disney did not live to see even the beginning of the creation of the park, originally spelled EPCOT Center when it opened on October 1, 1982, at a cost of $1.4 billion. But his plans for EPCOT detailed his vision of a self-contained community with all peoples working in harmony toward the common goal of a better world. Walt expressed this vision in the **City of the Future** model, which can be seen while riding Magic Kingdom's Tomorrowland Transit Authority. EPCOT would be a dynamic community, ever growing and changing to reflect the ongoing process of human and technological progress.

Most of the elements Walt intended for his utopian city were never implemented in the form he originally intended. However, we see his vision of a shopping, dining, and entertainment complex through the creation of Downtown Disney, a family-oriented sporting venue at ESPN's Wide World of Sports, and some of his ideas for a residential community in the nearby town of Celebration. The people-mover concept was realized in the WEDway People Mover (now called Tomorrowland Transit Authority) at Magic Kingdom; although it does not function as an interior park element, the monorail received the stamp of approval and now, appropriately, winds its way over Future World.

After Walt's death in 1966, the plans for EPCOT Center divided it into two separate, distinct parks, one showcasing the latest technology and the second a tribute to world cultures. After much grumbling and debate, one of the project Imagineers took the two park models, which were sitting near each other on a design table, and literally pulled everything together. From this one small act, a brand-new Walt Disney World theme park was born. And now, we have Epcot!

Future World

Attention to detail is the hallmark of Walt Disney Imagineering. From the color of the plants to the size, placement, and design of the buildings, every detail carries the theme throughout each attraction.

Future World represents both the living world on the right of the park and the world of innovation on the left, separated by Innoventions Plaza and the Fountain of Nations. Notice the smooth, curved lines of the curbs, pathways, rocks, and landscaping on the right of Future World and the more angular, well-defined lines on the left? Making the distinction between nature's flow and science's requirement to operate within specific lines is a small design element that enhances the complete theme.

In keeping with the spirit of a global community, the Innoventions Plaza's Fountain of Nations (known as Fountain of World Friendship when Epcot opened) contains **water** from rivers and bodies of water around the world, with a gallon from each having been added to the fountain on opening day as a gesture of peace and togetherness.

✳ Fascinating Fact

Curious about which bodies of water were included in the International Ceremony of the Waters? The water came from the Adriatic Sea, the Arctic Ocean, the Bodensee (which represents Switzerland, Germany, and Austria), the Caribbean Sea, the Cauca River in Columbia, the Cho Jong Yak Soo (an underground river in Korea), a sample of God's Water from the Ise Shrine near Osaka, Harrison Cave water from Barbados, Lake Geneva, Lake Inari in Finland, the Manzanares River in Spain, the Meuse River (which runs through

France, Belgium, and the Netherlands), mineral springs water of Sidi Ali in Morocco, the Mississippi and Nile rivers, the Philippine Sea, the River Thames, the Sea of Japan, the Seine, Senegambia River, Tivoli Gardens Lake in Denmark, Trevi Fountain, Xochimilco in Mexico City, the Yangtze River, and Zeplin Dam in the former Czechoslovakia. ✳

Now, standing on the pathway between Fountain of Nations and Mouse Gear, with the fountain to your right and the shop to your left, you will see two **drinking fountains** ahead of you. Take a drink and listen closely. Something is going on in there!

Spaceship Earth

The Imagineers strive to communicate their story effectively, making the attractions themselves a virtual playground of hidden magic. In the case of Spaceship Earth, the story is about communication. At least it was until a 2007 refurbishment. As you journey upward, you may notice an unintentional disconnect between the scenes that existed prior to the makeover and the ride's new story, which is now a more general observation of human innovation rather than communication.

Spaceship Earth is an astonishing structure in many ways, including the fact it was designed with a **runoff system** that prevents water from reaching the ground when it rains. Each panel funnels water away from the surface, eventually emptying into the World Showcase lagoon.

The Imagineers spared no effort in creating accurate scenes inside Spaceship Earth, right down to re-creating some of the actual musical instruments, documents, and machines that add an extra air of authenticity. In the Sistine Chapel scene, Michelangelo's **paint conveyer system** is a replica of the original, the **quadrant** in the Islamic scene (used for navigation and astronomy) is a replica of those used in the tenth century, and the **steam press** in the printing scene is a duplicate of a press designed by William Bullock in 1863.

As you pass the **cave dwellers scene**, take a quick flash photo of the wall directly to your right. You'll have a fun surprise when you see the picture later.

Many of us dream of reading an authentic letter written by an Egyptian pharaoh, and the Imagineers haven't failed us. The scrolls in the Egyptian scene duplicate real **documents written by a pharaoh** to one of his agents. If you've brushed up on hieroglyphic writing, you'll know the **hieroglyphics** throughout the Egyptian scene are accurate representations of real words.

Although the smell of burning wood may distract you, notice the graffiti on the walls as you pass by the sacking of Rome scene. It reproduces actual **graffiti** found in the Roman city of Pompeii.

Next up is the Renaissance. While guests will never have the opportunity to try it out, the movable type on the **printing press** in the scene really can move. Johann Gutenberg would also be delighted to know his likeness in the same scene is reading an exact reproduction of the original forty-two-line Gutenberg Bible. The page depicted in Spaceship Earth copies an original housed at the Henry E. Huntington Library in San Marino, California. Why the forty-two-line distinction? It refers to how many lines were printed on each page, not that the entire Bible consisted of only forty-two lines.

Renaissance citizens honored the beauty of the human form in their art, poetry, and song. Prior to the 2007 makeover of Spaceship Earth, the **nude female sculpture** was left bare, an entirely appropriate and accurate representation of the real thing. Apparently, she was deemed risqué and is now covered.

As you continue to spiral upward through Spaceship Earth, listen closely as you pass by the telegraph scene. Can you hear **Morse code**? The message being tapped out is the 1869 announcement that the golden spike linking the transcontinental railway at Promontory Peak has just been driven in.

Can you guess which scene could win a "Most Likely to Be Updated Again Soon" contest? It has to be the recently added computer room scene, with the **lab technician** dressed in a mini-skirt and go-go boots. Accuracy is usually paramount, but in this case, it may be hard to convince viewers the office dress code was *that* casual in the 1970s or 1980s!

Who is that **computer guy** sitting in the garage, inventing the personal computer? Think he might be Microsoft's Bill Gates or Apple's Steve Jobs or Steve Wozniak? Nope. The official Imagineer stance is that he is a compilation of everyone whose efforts went into creating PCs.

Imagine That!

Pam Fisher, Walt Disney Imagineer and senior show writer, says the garage scene is "an homage to all the young dreamers working out of their garages and on their kitchen tables, perfecting all the technologies needed to create the personal computer. Hewlett-Packard started in a garage. Apple started in a garage. But there were also many other nameless people in Northern California working in their own garages at the time, figuring out the other parts of the puzzle. This scene is a salute to them all."

Finally, as you descend back to terra firma and your future is decided via touch-screen technology, a perky voice cheerfully approves of your choices by saying, "**Looks like it's going to be a great big beautiful tomorrow**!" Visitors to Magic Kingdom's Carousel of Progress will recognize the reference to that attraction's theme song, "A Great Big Beautiful Tomorrow."

Universe of Energy

Turning to the left, or scientific, side of Future World, the Universe of Energy may be the most obviously educational attraction in Walt Disney World. It was originally a rather dry litany of potential energy sources, making the ride popular for a nap in air-conditioned comfort. A 1996 remake introduced the comedy of Ellen DeGeneres and the competitive thrill of popular television game show *Jeopardy!*, lightening the mood while focusing on the issue of sustainable fuel choices.

As you approach Universe of Energy, notice how the vertical columns are reminiscent of a **rainbow**. Before the pavilion's 1996 makeover, the color scheme was more in keeping with the energy theme, with panels running along each side starting as a warm sunshine yellow, gradually becoming fiery umber, like a beacon pointing toward a red-hot power center.

Speaking of heat, look up at the roof. It's covered with **80,000 photovoltaic cells** that provide solar energy, captured and converted into AC, and then used to power the ride. So, as the voiceover indicates during your journey, you are literally "riding on sunshine."

During the pre-show, when Ellen realizes she is losing badly at *Jeopardy!* but has control over the outcome because she's the one dreaming about it, she says, "**Freeze!**" Notice, however, her lips do not move. Oops!

Fans of the 1940 Disney movie *Fantasia* might recognize a small tribute to Walt's most ambitious cinematic undertaking as they travel past a confrontation between the *T. rex* and Stegosaurus. The same scene can be found in the movie's "Rite of Spring" composition, depicting the creation of the cosmos through to the dinosaurs' extinction.

As you exit the dinosaur portion of the ride, you hear a radio broadcast compliments of **KNRG News Radio**. Do the station's call letters bring anything to mind? They are a shortened version of "kinetic energy."

Mission: SPACE

The next pavilion, Mission: SPACE, holds the secret to space travel, providing an experience the average person could not have any other way. When the attraction originally opened, it was too much like the real thing. Although it's been toned down (and comes in two versions: Green, the noncentrifuge version, and Orange, the full-blown experience), it remains the only attraction in Orlando equipped with motion discomfort bags.

Take time to look around the Planetary Plaza (courtyard) before you enter. The walls are adorned with **plaques containing quotes** from well-known astronomers and astronauts, including Kalpana Chawla, one of the astronauts who died in the tragic explosion of the *Columbia* space shuttle in 2003.

The **gold spheres** scattered across the mockup of the moon in the Planetary Plaza represent each of the twenty-nine moon-landing missions sent up by the United States and the Soviet Union between 1959 and 1976.

Imagine That!

Developing attraction concepts isn't as simple as coming up with a terrific idea, especially when it requires new technology and financial backing. Mission: Space was one such attraction. Imagineer Eddie Sotto, senior vice president of Concept Design with WDI from 1986 to 1999, describes the process when he says the Imagineers wanted to "give the most accurate ride experience that would simulate a rocket launch, as that was what most guests were fascinated with when it came to Space. The funny thing about Mission: Space is that we really wanted management to know the ride experience was going to be unique. In order to get the funding to convince them, I had to lie on my back suspended between two chairs, facing the ceiling, making all manner of 'communications chatter' and engine noises, contorting my face to simulate the sustained G forces on my body. All in a business suit. Think Cirque du Soleil meets Apollo 13. Marty Sklar, WDI's president, enthusiastically decided to fund the development of the show, but thankfully never asked me to demonstrate the effect again!"

Once inside, look at the bottom of the large glass display panel as you line up for Mission: SPACE. The white **three letter / four number notations** along the bottom are initials of the Imagineers, designers, and contributors who worked on the creation of this amazing attraction.

See that **Horizons logo** in the center of the rotating gravity wheel in the queue? That was the name of the attraction located on the site that now houses Mission: SPACE. Horizons centered on possible future habitat options, including those in space.

Eight **Lunar Roving Vehicles** were constructed for NASA by Boeing, three of which were taken to the moon and remain there to this day. A fourth authentic Lunar Rover is on display here in the line, on loan from the Smithsonian in Washington, D.C.

Just before you pass into the Training Ops bay, notice the **number 42** painted above the doors. Perhaps it's a subtle reference to Douglas Adams's *The Hitchhiker's Guide to the Galaxy?* The answer to Life, the Universe, and Everything in Adams's book is, of course, the number 42.

Once in the Training Ops bay, you will see **Mission Control** on the right. Imagineers are both creative and economical, using retired attraction set pieces if they fit into a new attraction. Mission: SPACE has a number of pieces from the old Mission to Mars ride, formerly in Tomorrowland at Magic Kingdom. The controls, switches, lights, and monitors are all recycled from the former attraction. The gravity wheel is from the 2000 movie, *Mission to Mars*.

The **video monitors** showing guests enjoying Mission: SPACE actually display taped versions of the guest experience. Once you enter the ride pod, you will notice there are no cameras inside, which should come as some comfort to riders on the Orange version as they react to the intense centrifugal forces that make this ride so spectacular!

Before you board your spacecraft, you will have a briefing by someone who may look familiar. That's actor **Gary Sinise**, who played the part of Co-Commander Jim McConnell in the *Mission to Mars* movie. How appropriate!

Test Track

Right next door is the only place in the world where live guests are used as crash test dummies. Test Track also has the dubious distinction of being the ride most likely to break down, but when it's working, it's a real adrenalin rush!

Seat the kiddies in the back if you can, so their faces show up better in the ride photo.

Each car on Test Track is powered by three onboard computers. Working together, they have more processing power than the space shuttle. Each vehicle actually has an amazing twenty-two wheels (though guests only see four) and six braking systems.

Those **crash test dummies** you see as you walk through Test Track's line will have their necks bent, knees hit, and chests struck 720 times during the course of the day.

✳ Fascinating Fact

Some of the tests being inflicted upon the crash test dummies through Test Track used to be done on human volunteers, among them a professor at Wayne State University in Michigan, Lawrence Patrick. One of his students, Herald Mertz, was inspired by Professor Patrick and later became the creator of the Hybrid III crash test dummy, which is the standard dummy in use today. ✳

Giving a slight twist to the hidden Imagineer signature, many of the **pictures of children** you see as you are queuing are relatives of the attraction's designers.

"All work and no play . . ." has never been a problem for the Test Track crew. See if you can find various toys based on Disney movie characters scattered around the workbenches. They have a strange tendency to move from one workbench to another, compliments of some mischievous Cast Members, so keep a sharp eye out for them.

Once you're on the ride itself, just after the Suspension Test and Anti-Lock Brake Test, you will begin your Cornering Test. Notice the **mile markers**, which should read 000,

050, 100, and so on. The first mile marker indicates cattle crossing and reads M00.

Then, when you enter the heat chamber, look left. Someone is making breakfast, with **two eggs** frying on a bit of aluminum foil on the heat compressor. Those fun-loving Imagineers never miss a chance for a visual gag along the way! And there's another coming right up . . .

Midway into the cold chamber, look to your left again. See that blue ice-cube tray? **Icicles** apparently grow upward in Epcot, creating a cool treat after your trip through the heat chamber, perhaps?

Can you stand one more? Once inside the corrosion chamber, look at the bottom of the robots to either side of your car (the ones that spray you with a fine mist). Their ID letterings spell out **CRUS-T and RUS-T**.

Innoventions Plaza

Back in the center of Future World, Electric Umbrella is a great place for a quick lunch or a drink to beat the heat. Be sure to throw your rubbish in the trash bin marked **Waste Please** (usually next to the toppings bar where the condiments and burger fixings are located). Listen closely for a surprising commentary; you may hear children arguing over who gets the last of the fries!

Birds of the aggressive variety used to frequent the Walt Disney World outdoor dining locations. Why are they less pervasive at Epcot now? It is said the speaker systems play sounds of **birds in distress**, which keep hungry winged pests at bay. Many outdoor locations also use coverings or wires to discourage bird invasion, so although places like Electric Umbrella have nicely shaded outdoor dining, it's really there to keep the birds away.

✳ Fascinating Fact

Natural pest management is used throughout Walt Disney World. Disney releases 250,000 warrior insects—they get rid of harmful pests—each year, and even allows guests to take part via the Lady-bug Release at Epcot. Interestingly enough, feral cats also roam Disney property, working hard to keep the rodent population down. Look out, Mickey! ✳

Pass through the walkway between Innoventions West and the Fountain View Bakery, heading toward The Land Pavilion. Just beyond, you'll take a "walk through time" over the **Timeline of Discovery**. Look at the large circle below your feet with quotes from various scientists and inventors about their reflections on historical discoveries, such as the Phoenician invention of the alphabet, Heinrich Hertz's discovery of radio waves, the creation of the internal combustion engine by Jean-Joseph Étienne Lenoir, and the discovery of penicillin by Alexander Fleming.

Next, turn left and walk toward the restrooms. Before you reach them, you will see **two drinking fountains**. In an effort to keep hydrated, take a drink (or four!) from the taller fountain and listen closely. There's someone working in the pipes!

The Land

Crossing over to the "natural" side of Future World, the Land Pavilion draws guests in with sweeping mosaics along both sides of the walkway. The artist designed the mosaics as representations of the **layers of the earth**, exposed after a volcano eruption. The left and right mosaics are almost identical. There are two small differences: an emerald green tile has been placed in the right-hand mural (look for a gold band of tiles to the left of the sign, then look to the right end of the gold band), and a ruby red tile in the left-hand mural. Again, artists can't sign their work, so the tiles were placed to symbolize the artist's children's birthstones. Sadly, you won't find the red tile. It was stolen and never replaced.

Also notice the walkway as you make your way up to the pavilion's door. The pigmented pavement is an extension of the theme—in this case, of the creation of land—and is meant to represent **lava** flowing from a volcano. The red pavement is hot lava; the black is cooled lava.

✳ Fascinating Fact

All of the natural elements that went into creating the murals at the pavilion's entrance were made from materials found on Walt Disney World property. ✳

Look up when you enter Sunshine Season Food Fair inside the pavilion. Those **balloons** overhead represent Earth (in the middle), with the four seasons surrounding it. The green balloon represents spring, yellow for summer, orange for fall, and blue for winter. Some of the characters on each balloon honor various cultures around the world.

In keeping with Walt's vision for his city of tomorrow, **quotations** adorning the wall along the queue for the **Living with the Land** ride offer eloquent insights into humankind's relationship with the environment. As profound as they are, each quote comes from the unique perspective of the child who wrote it.

During your boat ride, note the **house number** on the mailbox as you pass through the farmhouse scene on the ride. It's #82, a subtle nod to 1982, the year EPCOT Center opened.

Then, when you reach the greenhouse area, watch for the **tomato tree**. It's a *Guinness Book of World Records* holder. The plant yielded a record-breaking 32,000 tomatoes in one year, a whopping 1,151.84 pounds!

✳ Fascinating Fact

Plants in the Living with the Land greenhouses are grown using a soil-free technique called hydroponics (hydro meaning water and ponic meaning labor). It seems like a high-tech method, but it has been around for centuries. Ancient hieroglyphs show the Egyptians grew plants in water; the Aztecs and Chinese created floating gardens; the hanging gardens of Babylon used hydroponics; World War II troops stationed in the Pacific without usable soil were fed partially through hydroponic systems; and later, even NASA got in on the act! ✳

If you dine at Sunshine Season Food Fair, Garden Grill, or at the Coral Reef Restaurant in the Seas with Nemo and Friends Pavilion, you will probably dine on foods grown in the Living with the Land attraction.

The pavilion's other big attraction Soarin', added more recently, was originally built at Disney's California Adventure park in Anaheim in 2001. As you watch the pre-flight video, notice the **flight number**. It is 5505, honoring Soarin's official opening at Epcot on May 5, 2005. Clever!

There is a stand of trees between the Land Pavilion and the Seas with Nemo and Friends Pavilion, worth a moment's notice in passing. If you are visiting in the autumn, you cannot miss the trees for their beautiful reddish-violet flowers. When they are not in bloom, look for the trees covered in thick spikes, just after you pass under the monorail to the right of the Seas entrance (they'll be right in front of you). You've found the *Chorisia speciosa*, native to Brazil and commonly known as the **floss-silk tree**, a name that gives away its unique charm. When the fruit of the tree bursts open, it releases a great puffball of seeds that glide on the breeze at the end of a silken floss. Why is this tree so appropriate to Epcot? Because the floss once performed a high-tech function as the filling for life preservers and pillows before the dawn of synthetic fibers.

The Seas with Nemo and Friends

Formerly known as the Living Seas before Nemo and friends made a big splash, the pavilion's emphasis was on the creation of the world's oceans and their abundance of life. The attraction's former storyline was simple; a documentary-style movie described the evolution of the seas, followed by a clever Hydrolator (simulated underwater elevator) journey to marine research center Sea Base Alpha. A quick Sea Cabs ride took guests to, and through, the pavilion's massive aquarium.

Sadly, during a refurbishment in 2005–2006, many of the attraction's wonderful hidden gems were covered or removed. Letters and numbers that once graced the main lobby area—a tribute of initials and birthdates of the Imagineers involved in creating the original attraction—were removed. **LS86**, a nod to the 1986 opening date of the Living Seas, has also been covered in the name of progress.

The Seas pavilion is the only place in Epcot where live animals are the feature attraction, but Walt Disney World's commitment to nature is still evident here. In fact, the first manatee born in captivity at Epcot's Living Seas Pavilion in 1991 was named **Chester**, which stands for Children Helping Endangered Species To Eventually Recover.

The saltwater aquarium was the largest in the world (Disney called it the "sixth largest ocean in the world") until Georgia opened its new aquarium in Atlanta in 2005. Still, if you skimmed just one inch of water off the top of the aquarium, you could fill an entire standard swimming pool.

Guests aren't likely to see what was once a real eye-catcher in the aquarium before caretakers separated the dolphins from their slower cohabitants. Ever playful, the dolphins took delight in ramming the sea turtles, sending them hurtling through the tank at great speed. A real stunner not only for the turtles but also for sharp-eyed guests, it is yet another attraction that has found its way into the annals of history at the Seas.

Turtle Talk with Crush, the delightful preschooler-oriented attraction that fascinates even the most jaded visitors, is currently the only area with a secret, and I'm not going to give this one away. If you are over the age of six, part of the show's fun is trying to figure out how Crush is so accurate with his wonderful banter. Without giving away the secret, it can be said that the technology is fairly complex, but the concept is simple. You can easily figure it out if you think about it.

Nemo can be found all around his new home at the Seas pavilion. As you walk through the queue toward your Clam-mobile (which replaced the Sea Cabs after the pavilion's redesign), notice the **beach signs** on the tall white signpost. If you look carefully at the advertisement for Daily Diving

Departures, you will notice they are provided by Nautical Exploration & Marine Observation, or N.E.M.O.

Imagination!

As you make your way toward World Showcase, you'll find the last of the Future World pavilions, Imagination, which is all about whimsy and the strange and wonderful places our imagination can take us with "just one spark."

Never satisfied with the obvious when a bit of ingenuity could be employed, the Imagineers have taken a twist on the waterfall concept. Look at the **water feature** as you walk toward the pavilion. The water isn't flowing downward; it's shooting upward, a mental nudge to viewers to allow their creativity to run wild.

You may recognize some of the names on the doors as you make your way through the Journey into Imagination with Figment queue. In particular, notice the door marked **Dean Finder**. When the Journey into Imagination Ride opened, the two main characters were a lovable purple Figment and Dreamfinder, the adventurer who created Figment. Dean Finder is a reference to the long-gone and much missed Dreamfinder.

Although nearly everyone agrees Figment is pretty cute, there is disagreement over whether he's a dragon or dinosaur. The truth is, he is neither. Dreamfinder conjured up the body of a lizard, the horns of a steer, and the nose of a crocodile, added wings, big, wide eyes, and "just one spark" of imagination, which came to life as Figment.

As you move into the upside-down room during your ride, notice the red and yellow paint pots. They're **Figment Pigments**, named after the attraction's mischievous mascot.

Imagine That!

During Epcot's 25th Anniversary Celebration, Disney Legend and international ambassador for Walt Disney Imagineering Marty Sklar said, "Walt's vision for Epcot really set the course for everything that has happened here at Walt Disney World in the forty-one years since. Those letters, E P C O T, have, in fact, been carried out through the E, Experimental, in everything from transportation systems to trash collection and even talking turtles; the P, Prototype, in energy systems, construction methods, and new entertainment experiences; the C, Community, on a peak day, right here on these 28,000 acres, there are more than 300,000 people, including the guests at our four parks, resort hotels, and campgrounds, and between 50–60,000 Cast Members, a community requiring all the services of a good size city, whether it's moving them, feeding them, housing them or entertaining them; and the T, Tomorrow. So many firsts, so many steps, large and small, into the future. So many dreams come true."

As you're leaving Future World for World Showcase, look at the hilly area just beyond the rose garden between the Imagination! Pavilion and Refreshment Port. Sometimes, especially during summer months, you will see a **small robotic contraption** moving across the grassy hill. It's a solar-powered lawn mower!

World Showcase

The layout of the international pavilions that make up this half of the park is well established. The original concept placed the U.S.A. Pavilion at the front of World Showcase (in what is now Showcase Plaza) with near-neighbors Mexico and Canada bordering on either side. Guests would walk through an archway into World Showcase, with the main attraction, The American Adventure, housed in a building situated above the archway. Ultimately it was decided America should "play host to the World," and the pavilion was centered at the back. Mexico and Canada remain in their originally intended positions.

Imagine That!

If you enjoyed looking for three bathtubs in Magic Kingdom, you have another challenge here in World Showcase. Can you find the small replica of the giant dolphin perched on top of the Dolphin Resort (let's just admit it really looks like a fish) somewhere in World Showcase? It's not hidden, but it's not where you might expect it to be. Give it your best effort, but if you don't find it, go ahead and cheat by looking at Solution 3 in Appendix B.

There are currently eleven pavilions that make up World Showcase. It seems impossible to imagine more than one or two new ones in the future, but there is actually room for seven more!

A curiosity as you walk toward Mexico from Showcase Plaza again highlights the attention to detail Disney Imagineers bring to their work. Once you pass the shop in Showcase Plaza, begin looking toward the Morocco Pavilion. Does something look slightly out of place? What appears to be a Moroccan building far off in the distance is actually the top of the **Tower of Terror** at Disney's Hollywood Studios. When the Imagineers realized you could see the tower from Epcot, they included stylized minarets on the roof to help the tower blend more harmoniously with the Moroccan theme.

Mexico

As authentic as it looks at first glance, the Mexico Pavilion's pyramid actually represents three distinct cultures. The pyramid architecture is **Mayan**, with one temple built at the top rather than two, as would be seen on an Aztec pyramid. The décor is **Aztec**, with brightly colored murals and menacing heads guarding the entry. Many of the design elements throughout are representative of **Toltec** art. The pyramid itself is a representation of an **Aztec temple of Quetzalcoatl**. Each serpent head symbolizes Quetzalcoatl, son of the Creator God. Appropriately enough, the **Fire God altar** at the top of the pyramid is used as a launch location for some of IllumiNations' fireworks. Aztec mythology indicates Quetzalcoatl was, among other things, the bringer of chocolate to humans. Pop in to Plaza de los Amigos for a sweet treat and give a nod of thanks to this benevolent Aztec god!

Imagineers originally intended guests to walk through what is now the small **jungle area** to the right of the pyramid (where the disabled entrance is now located). However, many guests could not find the door so it was relocated to the front.

Doesn't that big **slab of art** look out of place on the front of the pyramid? When the pavilion was created, guests could not resist the temptation to climb the steps for that "special picture," putting themselves in harm's way and giving the Cast Members (and Disney lawyers!) fits. Imagineers added the artwork in an effort to make the steps inaccessible, thus avoiding possible disaster.

Why is it always twilight inside Mexico's Plaza de los Amigos? Because twilight is the time friends and family—relationships central to Mexican culture—gather in the plaza for socializing.

Animales Fantasticos, the colorful wooden figures being carved in the lobby of the pavilion, are an ancestral Zapotec art form in Oaxaca (pronounced "Wa-HAH-ca"), Mexico. Known as *alebrijes*, the magical creatures hold a special secret. Because the artist puts such intense effort into the work, it is believed the piece carries part of the carver's being forever.

It wasn't meant to be a secret, but most guests overlook the large contraption to the left of the Kidcot station. In fact, it is both a **postcard creator** and a rare free souvenir. Choose from a selection of comical animated scenes, record yourself or your group hamming it up for the camera, then e-mail your postcard to friends and family for a unique (and hilarious) memento of your trip to Epcot.

Remember the **floss-silk tree** over by the Land Pavilion and the Living Seas? A companion has found a home in its native land. Look for the trees with thick spines in the landscaped area to the left of the pyramid's entry stairway.

Norway

The buildings throughout the Norway Plaza mimic the architectural design styles traditionally found in Oslo, Alesund, Bergen, and the Setesdal Valley, from rough and rustic to a neat, tidy style that would not seem out of place along the New England coastline. Even better, this is one of only two World Showcase pavilions (the other is Mexico) that boast a ride!

Norway's Restaurant Akershus, serving up traditional Norwegian fare, is based on Oslo's medieval **castle Akershus**, originally built in 1299. It was renovated extensively from 1637 through 1648, when it took on the style of the castle we see today.

Traditionally built with dovetailed joints, **Norway's medieval stave churches** (in this case, the Gol Stave Church originally built in Hallingdal) are faithfully reproduced, supposedly without the benefit of iron nails. But a close inspection not only sets that idea to rest, it also reveals the church is built mostly of fiberglass! However, the base is built on stone in recognition of the rain and humidity encountered in Florida, which would make the traditional wood flooring rot.

Even more peculiar is the fact the church represents a **Christian church**, but it honors Nordic gods! The original stave (meaning "pillar") churches are believed to have been built on Norse holy grounds, with their temples torn down and replaced by Christian churches around 1000 A.D.

While the Imagineers remained faithful to **traditional roofing material** when they designed Kringla Bakeri Og Kafe, the classic goat-on-the-roof to keep the grass trimmed was not practical. Instead, dedicated gardeners hand-trim it using small shears.

Mickey Mouse couldn't resist sailing with the Vikings. Look for the **hidden Mickey** in the giant mural in the loading area for the Maelstrom ride. No cheating . . . he's there if you look closely (and figure out the hint just given!). If you can't find him, his location is given in Solution 4 in Appendix B.

Are you ready for a treasure hunt of sorts? There are twenty-eight mischievous little **trolls** hiding throughout the pavilion, some as singles and some in pairs. See how many you can find! You'll find their locations in Appendix B, Solution 5, but give it a try on your own first. Take note, they just appeared one day in March 2008, and they may disappear just as quickly. It's possible they'll only come out of hiding during the annual

Flower and Garden Festival, which runs from mid-March through the beginning of June.

China

From Norway, we journey to Asia, where the China Pavilion's Temple of Heaven, a true one-half-scale representation of the Beijing Temple, is filled with symbolism. Built as a place of prayer for a successful harvest, each element has meaning, with a surprising secret in the heart of the temple. Look at the floor as you walk through the front doors. The **concentric circles** move inward in multiples of three (three symbolizing living or giving life, and also the trinity of Heaven, Earth, and Man in Chinese numerology) until they reach the center circle. Stand with your feet directly over the circle and say something, anything. The building is acoustically perfect, causing your voice to vibrate directly back into your ears. Step outside the circle, even just one step, and speak again. Notice the difference? You can whisper as you stand over the circle and still have the effect of hearing your voice as it bounces back to you. Notice how it sounds slightly different from the way you hear it inside your head.

Looking progressively upward, the temple's four columns represent the four seasons; the square beams represent Earth; the round beams depict the heavens; and the twelve pillars are representative of the twelve months of the Chinese year.

Two recurring themes are the **phoenix and the dragon**, representing the empress and the emperor, respectively. Notice some dragons have only four fingers. They represent masculinity in general; in a spiritual context, such as here in the temple, they are the generators of wind and rain, aptly placed in a temple of prayer for abundant crops. Only the five-fingered dragon represents the emperor.

Detailed tiles inside the Temple of Heaven have an air of authenticity, and with good reason. Hundreds of tiles from the original temple have been faithfully re-created by the Imagineers.

✳ Fascinating Fact

Have you noticed the Kidcot Fun Stops at each of Epcot's pavilions? They debuted during the Millennium Celebration, when the Tapestry of Nations parade was running. Children (and adults who could not resist) could create a mask, adding various details to it in each pavilion, and then use it as they marched with the parade. When the Millennium Celebration ended, Tapestry of Nations became Tapestry of Dreams before it ended in March 2003. ✳

Other animals play an important role in Chinese culture. The **Foo Dog** (originally called "Dog of Fo") is the guardian and protector of sacred buildings and the defender of law. At Epcot's China Pavilion, both male and female Foo Dogs guard the entry to the Yong Feng Shangdian Department Store. Which is which? The male always has his foot on a globe; the female always has her foot on a baby Foo.

Another characteristic is one has its mouth open to attract positive spirits and good fortune, and the other has a closed mouth, meant to keep evil spirits at bay.

Browse through Yong Feng Shangdian, and you may discover a **weathered copper bowl** with handles on each side that sits on a pedestal near the back of the shop. It has a few inches of water in it, but it isn't obvious what its purpose might be. Here's the secret: Dip your finger in the water and rub it in a circle around the bowl rim. You need to use a little pressure (but not too much!), as you would do when making a wineglass sing. The bowl will sing, but it will do something else that is quite extraordinary when done correctly. Vibrations from your finger will cause the water to ripple, and then suddenly jump and splash! If you cannot get it to work, ask one of the shop assistants to show you how it's done.

As you stroll through China, you may notice the predominant color is red, which is considered lucky. Red is a color of happiness and prosperity, and it is also used to scare off certain evil spirits.

At the end of each ornate upward-tilting roofline, you will see a small character on the back of a chicken (yes, it's a chicken!). That's evil **Prince Min of the state of Qi**, ruler of China, who was hung from his ancestral temple's rooftop in 238 B.C. at the command of the prime minister. Superstition dictates a representation of Prince Min sitting on the roof will protect that building from evil spirits. As added insurance, he is guarded by helpful animals that line up behind him keeping watch. The number of animals guarding Prince Min indicates the status of that particular building.

The courtyard between the Temple of Heaven and Lotus Blossom Café, called **Xing Fu Jie** (Street of Good Fortune), is purposely narrow to give the crowded feeling you would have visiting a marketplace in China. A small detail, but highly effective.

Outpost

After you leave China, take a short diversion into the Africa-themed Outpost, just across the bridge. On the way, notice how this particular **bridge** crosses a waterway that extends beyond guest view. The bridge is unique in that it actually opens. Why? In part, because the barges and large globe employed during IllumiNations used to be stored just beyond the bend. When the globe first went into use, it made a dramatic entry via the waterway.

Pop into the Refreshment Outpost for a cooling beverage. While you're there, find another invigorating treat (sort of!) by opening the **Coca-Cola coolers**. It's a quirky secret, but, when it's working, it has real Kodak Moment potential, so have cameras ready (but not in the hands of the cooler opener)!

Also, look inside the Traders Hut. In one corner you'll see a cluster of elongated gourd-like vessels, hanging up near the ceiling. They're made from the fruit of the **sausage tree**, and you'll see them growing naturally when you visit Animal Kingdom.

Germany

As you stroll from pavilion to pavilion, each one captures your imagination in a different way. Many visitors feel Germany in particular has something just a bit special about it. The theme here feels familiar and homey, perhaps due to all those Brothers Grimm fairytales we heard as children, many of which have their roots in Germanic folk stories.

If you've ever visited Germany and recall that there are four **Hapsburg princes** on the facade of the Kaufhaus in Freiburg (on which Epcot's Das Kaufhaus is based), you'd be correct. Why are there only three here? Because there wasn't room to place all four of them on the ledge and still maintain the illusion of size through forced perspective, so only Philip I, Charles V, and Ferdinand I made the final cut.

Speaking of the Hapsburg princes, one of them has a **special jewel in his crown**. Look closely and you will see Mickey's likeness (the distinctive three circles that make up his head and ears) on the front of the left-most prince's crown.

The sixteen painted **coats of arms** adorning the front façade outside Sommerfest and the Biergarten Restaurant represent Germany's sixteen regions. Situated in the Hesse region, Frankfurt's coat of arms is the red and white lion on a blue background, just under the right-hand flower box over the entrance. It represents the connected building just to the left, which is styled after one of Frankfurt's most famous landmarks, the medieval Haus Römer (city hall) in Römerberg plaza.

Duck your head into the Volkskunst (folk art) shop. Pinned to the doorframe next to the Kidcot station, you'll see a cute cartoon of Theodore "Teddy" Roosevelt, the United States' twenty-sixth president, cuddled up with a bear cub. President Roosevelt is said to be the inspiration for the term **teddy bear**. Clifford Berryman, a political cartoonist, drew several cub cartoons after he heard about President Roosevelt's refusal to shoot an elderly bear during a hunting trip. His cartoons became famous and often featured the loveable cubby you see here at Epcot.

Just to the right of the Germany Pavilion, you'll find a charming addition that provides endless fascination for children in particular. The **train setup** is a captivating representation of a German-style town. However, there are times when the little town and its trains would fit more comfortably in Japan. As you peruse the pretty dwellings, you may see several would-be Godzillas perched on rooftops or in gardens, in the form of Florida's ever-present geckos. They're an unintended detail, but one that makes for a funny photo in your vacation scrapbook.

Italy

Much of the Italy Pavilion is based on the timeless city of Venice. The small canal at the front, as you walk toward the lagoon, represents the **famous waterways** and Grand Canal. There is a feeling of elegant simplicity and impressive, imposing power.

The Doge's Palace is beautiful indeed, but the palace in Venice also has a darker side. Deep inside the palace lays a prison and torture chamber, where enemies of the state endured interrogation. The infamous lover, Casanova, was incarcerated there, until his escape to Paris in 1756.

St. Mark's Square's distinctive **Lion of St. Mark**, statue of **St. Theodore and the Dragon**, and the square's landmark **Campanile** have all been faithfully reproduced. Real gold leaf covers the angel on top of the bell tower, which is somewhat of a departure for Disney designers, who typically afford less attention to the details guests will never see up-close.

Now look at the size of the bricks used to build the Campanile (bell tower). They are larger at the bottom, progressively getting smaller toward the top to give the illusion of height—another good example of forced perspective.

The **columns** along the Doge's pink and white marble palace—in this case, fiberglass over brick—hold (literally) an interesting secret. Look at the figures at the top of each column. They alternately hold a sword and an orb, with the orb held to the figure's side. This alternating pattern does not vary. Notice the three corner columns, however; the figure holding the orb has changed. The end-column figure holds a flattened orb in front of him. Although the real palace columns depict people, animals, and virtues, they do not feature the orb and sword symbols. Disney may have chosen these icons, which usually represent power and the world, because they are universal symbols without the moral messages contained in the palace's real icons.

A striking sculpture toward the back of the pavilion is a replica of the **statue of Neptune**, god of the sea. It isn't an exact copy; instead it is representative of many Italian fountains. Neptune holds a conch shell in one hand, which Roman mythology cites as the instrument used to herald his approach, and a trident in the other hand, the symbol of his power as a god. However, the dolphins on either side are not the animal Neptune is usually associated with. His typical companions would be horses or seahorses. Why is Neptune flanked by dolphins here? Legend has it he fell in love with the beautiful water nymph Amphitrite, but she refused his offer of marriage. He sent a dolphin as his ambassador; it convinced Amphitrite that the union would be a good one. As a reward for securing his bride, Neptune immortalized the dolphin in the heavens as the constellation Dolphinus.

Notice the **olive tree** next to the bridge over the Venice canal on the left as you face the pavilion? It was unexpectedly required to be trimmed to ten feet high as it was transported from Sacramento to its new home in Orlando. You can see where the old growth ends and new growth begins in several places. Some branches are smaller than the stump of a branch they grew out of and some just split off older branches, where cuttings are in evidence.

The American Adventure

Welcome, one and all, to the United States of America! Situated as the central pavilion in World Showcase, the American Adventure plays host to all the countries surrounding her, spreading her architectural arms wide in a gesture of hospitality. The spaciousness afforded to the pavilion and inclusion of the American Gardens Theater serve to high-light Walt Disney's pride in his country and his desire to share her bounty with all nations.

Although the imposing structure will probably catch your attention straight away, there is a greater feat of engineering here. Unfortunately, you cannot see it. Surprisingly, Magic Kingdom isn't the only park with underground **utili-dors**. As you walk toward the pavilion, notice how the land slopes upward. The attraction is actually on the second floor. There is literally a ground floor (in this case, an underground floor) below that houses the Audio-Animatronic scenes in the American Adventure show when they are not on stage.

Now, I'll let you in on another little secret if you promise not to make a nuisance of yourself when you check it out. See the **Fife and Drum Tavern** in front of the American Adventure? It just appeared one day. How could that happen? Well . . . designate one person in your group to quietly tap on the wall. Rather hollow sounding for a solid brick building, isn't it?

Many special touches are secrets because guests don't necessarily know what they mean even when they see them. Some are even more obscure, as they are completely overlooked until someone points them out. With that in mind, take a look at the clock at the top of the U.S.A. Pavilion, specifically the **numerals on the face**. Can you tell which one is unusual? The numeral 4 is presented as IIII (rather than IV) as would have been typical of the colonial period. The clock in Liberty Square at Magic Kingdom has the same numeral representation, in keeping with that Land's time period.

The U.S.A. Pavilion is another example of **forced per-spective**, and this time you can play an active part in bringing the secret to light. Stand in front of the building so you have a view from top to bottom. The building looks two stories high, with a cupola on top, but it isn't. It is actually five stories! In keeping with the requirement that colonial buildings were never more than two stories, forced perspective was used to create the illusion of a shorter building while providing the height needed above the American Adventure stage. You can see this technique more clearly if one person in your group walks to the front door. The doors look normal from a distance, but when someone stands in front of them you can see they are enormous. In fact, they are twelve feet tall!

All the flowers planted and potted around the pavilion are chosen to reflect the color scheme of **red, white, and blue**. You may have noticed the same patriotic palette over in Liberty Square in Magic Kingdom.

Imagine That!

Walt Disney's legacy is a big torch to carry, and something WDI does bear in mind as it designs new shows and attractions. Says Imagineer Eric Jacobson, "It's pretty daunting because he was such a creative genius. Walt was always looking forward and he said, 'Disneyland will never be finished as long as there is imagination left in the world.' Walt was the first to change things. He wanted to try things, and if it worked, he kept it. If it didn't work, he took it out and changed it. We want to honor the legacy of Walt Disney and everything he's done, but we also want to recognize the progressive nature of what he did. That's what we all have taken from him, is that we keep moving forward, keep trying new things, and keep experimenting. Hopefully we 'hit most of them out of the park,' but if there's something better that comes along, well, why not? Let's give a new generation something new to experience. Let's keep the heritage, but also celebrate the future."

Ready for something truly bizarre? When you enter the U.S.A. Pavilion's rotunda, walk to the corner of the room, to the left of the front doors. Among the original paintings adorning the walls, you will find a painting of a **World War II B-17 bomber**. Stand parallel to the painting and walk its length, watching the bomber as you walk. Notice how it seems to follow you? Go ahead . . . walk back and forth a few times to give your eyes time to adjust to the perspective. No matter which side you start from, the bomber will turn, always pointing in your direction.

Now look at the artist's signature on the bottom right of the painting. Imagineer R. Tom Gilleon was able to sneak his name into the work in two places. If you look closely, the box in the bottom right corner has **T. Gilleon** painted on it in red. Now look at the aircraft. Sharp eyes will make out **RTG82**, the artist's initials and the year he painted the picture. Although Imagineers are not usually allowed to sign their work, once the rotunda paintings were complete, an exception was made to place a formal signature on the paintings. Another curious fact about this work is that not all the mechanics are men. Most of the men had gone to war during that time and women were the ones working in the factories.

But that isn't the only fascinating picture, although it does have the most unusual perspective. Each of the rotunda's pictures has its own surprising inclusions. Walk to the back of the rotunda along the left-hand wall, to the painting titled *Lesson for the Future*, which has a tie to the Magic Kingdom. Can you figure out how? That book the teacher is reading is a story brought to life in Adventureland. Look closely and you can just make out the title, *Swiss Family Robinson.*

Turn around again and the first painting along the back wall, *Staying the Course*, has two hidden signatures of sorts. Michael Lloyd signed his own name on the sailboat's bell and placed his wife's name, Elaine, upside-down on the life-boat . . . twice!

Also along the back wall, the only painting not done by a Disney Imagineer is the NASA-themed *Reaching for the Stars*. Artist Robert McCall, who has been capturing the drama of space exploration on canvas for more than thirty-five years, created the montage here in Epcot. It accurately recreates the NASA patch on the astronaut's flight suit and the original space shuttle fuel tank, painted white (it is now left an unpainted orange, since the amount of paint needed to cover it added significant weight). The two astronauts are John Young and Bob Crippen, who piloted the first orbital test flight of the space shuttle, with John Young acting as the flight's commander. Another fascinating tidbit? That man in the green shirt in the lower right corner is Eugene Francis "Gene" Krantz, former flight director for NASA, who wrote the book, *Failure Is Not an Option*. He was instrumental in saving the crew during the *Apollo 13* crisis.

Two other portraits, *Building a Future Together* (the last painting on the far right of the back wall) and *Seeds of Hope* (across the rotunda, to the left of the front doors as you face them from inside), honor the contributions of Native Americans who, as depicted in the first painting, helped build America's skyscrapers. In the second picture, they are showing European settlers how to farm in the New World. The kneeling man teaching the pilgrims to use fish as fertilizer is none other than Tisquantum, better known as Squanto.

But the real heartstring puller is yet to come, after you enter the theater.

The patriotic American Adventure show, located on the second floor in the pavilion, requires guests to walk up a flight of stairs from the lobby. The staircase walls and ceiling are adorned with real **flags**, some easily recognized, others more obscure, but all having flown over the United States at some point in history. The banners in the middle row are American flags, including a version of a George III flag, the Betsy Ross flag, and the current U.S. flag. Other flags are from the Revolutionary War or countries that laid claim to some area of land before it became the United States. As you ascend, look for the white flag emblazoned with a large red X. That's the **Spanish Bourbon**, the oldest flag in the bunch, dating back to 1513.

Looking for the **elevator**? It's hidden behind a false door near the main front doors in the rotunda. Obviously, there were no elevators in colonial America, so covering it helps preserve an authentic representation of the theme.

Before you enter the theater, take a quick peek at the last portrait on the right-hand wall that looks like it could be a Norman Rockwell painting. The woman in green with her back to you is Imagineer and Disney Legend **Harriet Burns**, the first woman hired in a creative capacity rather than as office staff by WED Enterprises (later called Walt Disney Imagineering).

Once inside the theater, you'll see several lifelike statues in alcoves along the wall. Pay particular attention to the **farmer**. Imagineer and sculptor Blaine Gibson created the statue in the likeness of his father, who was a farmer by trade.

As you watch the stirring American Adventure show, notice how strictly the producer adhered to a realistic time frame. At the start, the cinematic elements are **paintings**; post–Civil War, they become **photographs**; and, by the dawn of the twentieth century, they are **moving pictures**.

In one of the show's more poignant scenes, a family is divided in their loyalty, with brother fighting against brother. Pay attention to the two young men standing at the back of the family portrait in this scene. They are Disney Imagineers Jeff Burke and John Olson.

Japan

Arriving in Japan, the main building—strikingly similar to Yakushiji Temple, one of the Seven Great Temples in Nara—sets a graceful tone. Warm wood and clean, flowing lines combine simplicity with timeless beauty.

Though it does not look out of place, most of the landscaping is not native to the country, as the Florida climate would not support indigenous plants. The enormous bunya-bunya tree near Yakitori House is actually native to Australia and is a close relative to the *Araucaria araucana*, or **monkey-puzzle** tree, which is native to Chile and Argentina. So why is it in Japan? Mostly for looks, but if you make the stretch it does fit here, as the monkey-puzzle is used in the art of bonsai for its lovely, cascading effect. Covered in prickly spikes, the full-grown bunya-bunya's cones can weigh 15 pounds!

Situated in front of Yakitori House, to the left of the Mitsukoshi store, Japan's **goju-no-to** (literally, five-storied pagoda) is five tiers high, with single tiers representing Earth,

Wind, Fire, Water, and Sky—the elements from which Buddhists believe all things are made.

The **temple bell** hanging from the corner would traditionally have been placed there to ward off evil spirits. Apparently, they don't like noise! Oddly enough, this particular bell never makes a sound when it blows in the wind, since it doesn't have a clapper.

✳ Fascinating Fact

What is that sticky goodness Japan's candy-artist Miyuki weaves into fancifully detailed animals? It's brown rice toffee and the technique she uses to create her masterpieces is the 2,400-year-old art of amezaiku, a rare art, practiced by only a handful of craftspeople. Miyuki is the world's only female amezaiku artist, having learned the technique from her grandfather. Make time to see her at the small kiosk near the front entry to the Mitsukoshi store. She makes several appearances a day. ✳

The pagoda's **roof ornament**, called a sorin—meaning Set of Treasures—holds great religious symbolism. The discs represent six elements: Hoju, the Sacred Jewel (wish fulfilling); Ryusha, the Dragon Wheel (a vehicle for angels to come to earth); Suien, the Water Flame (a charm to protect the pagoda against fire); Kurin, the Nine Rings (which represent Buddhist deities); Fukabachi, the Lotus Flower (spiritualism, purity, and the realization of life); and Roban, the Inverted Bowl (consciousness and the heavens). Who knew a decorative piece could be so profound? The sorin also traditionally works as a **stabilizing system** for the pagoda and, curiously enough, as a lightning rod.

Compare the **gardens** in Japan with those of China. Japan's gardens are active and moving, with a strong human influence. The Japanese believe you should recognize the work and intent of the gardener when you see the outcome. China's gardens are quiet, tranquil, with a feeling of timelessness as if nature, rather than the hands of humans, created them.

Original plans for the Japan Pavilion included a **Mount Fuji roller coaster** ride, which was scrapped for two related reasons. First, there was the matter of funding, and second, the pavilion's sponsor, Kodak, would certainly not want the name Fuji on their pavilion lest it remind guests of competitor, Fuji Film.

The large doors at the back that enter into the fortress (housing the Bijutsu-kan Gallery) were the original entry to the proposed attraction. Look to either side as you pass through and you'll see two large **samurai on horseback**.

There are many peaceful elements in Epcot, but one of the most mesmerizing can be found in Japan. On the right of the pavilion, you'll hear the tinkling, clacking, flowing sound of a **Shishi Odoshi**, or water hammer (usually displayed only in warmer months). As with all things Japanese, it is a practical item made beautiful, full of symbolism, and soothing to the soul. From a purely functional standpoint, however, they were originally used to scare deer out of the rice paddies.

A moment of reflection may be appropriate as you look at the torii gate situated in the World Showcase Lagoon. Its design is based on the Shinto **Itsukushima Shrine** torii gate in Hiroshima Bay. The original is a Japanese treasure built in the sixth century and reconstructed to its present form. It is unique in that it appears to be floating on the water when the tide is in. Torii gates represent the gateway between the physical and spiritual worlds. Placed outside Shinto shrines, where nature spirits are the focus of worship, the gates indicate holy ground. Traditionally, they are built in three parts (three being a sacred number).

Apparently the tide is always out in World Showcase Lagoon. Look at the legs of the torii gate and you will see there are **barnacles** clinging to the pillars. Just a little hint at how far out the tide goes in Hiroshima Bay, where visitors can walk out to the gate at low tide—but that's not going to happen in Epcot!

Storks are encouraged to nest on the roofs of homes and businesses in Japan, as they are believed to bring good luck. To that end, the rooftops here are painted blue, with **carved golden fish** on each end, in the hope a stork will be fooled into thinking they are nesting near water.

Imagine That!

Is it all blue-sky and smooth sailing at WDI? Nope! Imagineer Eric Jacobson talks about the excitement inherent in problem-solving. "We're constantly coming up with creative challenges and one thing I love is a challenge that seems insurmountable, and coming up with a solution that everybody says, 'That seems so logical,' but it wasn't that easy to get there. Walt Disney said, 'It's kind of fun to do the impossible' and that's what we live by every day. One of the moments that exemplifies that best is the idea for Blizzard Beach. We had four or five ideas that we were kicking around in our brain-storming meeting. One of the Imagineers drew a picture of an Alpine resort and said, 'What if we do a Bavarian kind of water park?' We said, 'Well, that's really crazy, to do a ski resort,' and at the same time, we said, 'How would you pull that off in Florida? It's certainly not cold and it would certainly be difficult to have snow.' In the meantime another Imagineer drew a picture of an alligator on skis and wrote underneath it, Ski Florida. We looked at that drawing and then at the other one with the Alpine theme and said, 'What a great idea, to have a snowstorm in Florida! But because it's in Florida it's constantly melting and that's the reason it would be a water park.' It's one of those things that is just so wacky and so off the wall that it's got to work. We probably brainstormed for three days, and then, within five minutes, those two things came together and became Blizzard Beach. Those kinds of examples are things you can struggle with, and, when you get the right idea, it's pretty obvious."

You may be tempted to believe the carved golden fish here are the dolphin you're searching for in the challenge I presented you with when you entered World Showcase. Remember, although it looks like a fish, it's really a dolphin, so these aren't what you're looking for. Keep going!

Enter the **Mitsukoshi** store through the back entrance and, as you walk through the store, you will be taking a trip forward in time. Wares in the back are ancient crafts (pottery, textiles) and become more modern as you browse toward the front, where children's pop-culture anime items are found. The original Mitsukoshi is Japan's oldest department store, dating back 335 years. It was originally called Echigoya and sold only kimonos. The store gradually expanded to include everyday items until it earned the title the "Harrods of Tokyo" and is now known for having the widest variety of stock and friendliest shop assistants in Asia. Epcot's Mitsukoshi maintains that reputation for quality and politeness in fine style.

Morocco

Morocco is one of Epcot's most beautiful pavilions, full of vibrant colors and startling patterns. It was important to the sponsors that traditional artistic customs be honored; hence they used their own artists to create the thousands of tiles and carvings you see.

As you enter the pavilion, look at the Arabic writing over the entry to Tangierine Café, to the right of the courtyard. Think it refers to the café? Nope! It reads, **Tourist Information**.

The prayer tower at the front of the pavilion is a replica of the twelfth-century **Koutoubia Minaret**, the first thing visitors see when they visit Marrakech. The original minaret stands 226 feet tall, and each of its arches and facades is different.

Pay close attention to the architecture. If you start at the back, it takes you from ancient history to more modern-day building styles, as would be typical in Moroccan cities. The architecture toward the back is representative of a castle around which the city would have grown, becoming progressively more modern farther from the castle.

The beautifully adorned gate standing proudly in the center is styled after the Bab Boujeloud, the original gate in Fez, which leads to the Medina, meaning "old city." Surprisingly, the original gate is not very old. It was built in 1913.

Because Muslims believe no one is perfect but Allah, there are **intentional design flaws** throughout the pavilion, though none take away from the overall grace and timelessness characteristic of Moroccan art. Look for these flaws as you admire the tile work. You'll find an example if you walk through the front door of the Fez House, pass the first two pillars, turn left, and look at the second pillar in that left-side row. See the big blue–and–yellow star design? Look just above and to the right of it. A black-and-white pattern has been modified slightly by the use of a pale blue tile.

You'll know you've reached the **Fez House** when you enter the small courtyard decorated almost entirely in tiles. The upper story is the homeowner's living quarters. If you stop and listen, you'll hear the family inside (wait for it!). Apparently a guest has shown up unannounced and the family is bustling about to get refreshments. If you pay close attention, you may hear the tea service hit the floor when one of the children trips over another in their haste to set out a snack. Stand there long enough and you'll hear the English-speaking guest arrive.

Restaurant Marrakech holds a true historical treasure. Morocco was the first country to acknowledge the United States as a country, establishing what would become a long friendship. A replica of **His Majesty Mohamed III's** correspondence with President George Washington is framed on the wall in the restaurant's waiting area.

Some elements in the pavilion were created by Disney's own artists rather than those brought in by the Moroccan government, and, although they don't often get things wrong, they certainly goofed in this case. As you face the entry to Restaurant Marrakech, turn to the left and walk toward the bend in the pathway. Along the upper wall is a series of pointers. While they are accurate in their look and spacing, Disney designers completely missed the boat in regards to their use. What are they? **Sundials.** But they were placed in a location that doesn't catch the sun, thus rendering them useless.

There is a small, attractive fountain to the right of the restaurant entrance. Stand there for a few minutes and you may hear a **conversation from within the shop** behind you. The merchant and one of his patrons are discussing some of the shop's items.

In the same location, you'll hear other sounds of everyday life. Particularly enchanting are the **singing children**, happily chiming out a song about their school life and lessons, just as they do in real-life Morocco.

Out of respect for Muslim spiritual beliefs, the Moroccan Pavilion does not light up during IllumiNations. If you find a location that gives you a view of the pavilion, you'll see it only as a dark spot, in contrast to the other pavilions, which are framed in white lights.

Then, as you walk toward France, notice how the color of the pathway changes. As always, there's a reason, and in this case it's because the darker pigment represents the **Strait of Gibraltar**. You are symbolically crossing the thin body of water between the Atlantic Ocean and the Mediterranean Sea. However, if you had really crossed the strait from Morocco, you'd end up in Spain, not France. Fuel for the ongoing assertion Epcot will someday have a Spain pavilion? You be the judge!

France

Imagineers strive to create realistic settings, remaining true to the experience you would have when traveling abroad. Usually the inspiration is taken from real life. That is certainly the case here in the France Pavilion.

In the case of the **park bordering the canal** along the pavilion, it is true life as seen through the eyes of the artist Georges Seurat. Imagineers were inspired by his painting, *A Sunday Afternoon on the Island of La Grande Jatte*, when they were creating the park.

France's iconic **Eiffel Tower** is also another beautiful example of forced perspective. To maintain the illusion of a thousand-foot tower within the confines of Epcot, the one you see here is built to one-tenth scale and is meant to be viewed as if far away. Because Disney usually does not build, paint, or embellish things guests will never see, you can guess what they decided to do (or in this case, not do) with the bottom of the tower.

To further maintain the illusion, Epcot's Eiffel Tower has **deterrents** to prevent birds from landing on it. If they were allowed to perch there, the tower would visually shrink while the birds would look colossal!

✳ Fascinating Fact

It may be delicious when used as a flavoring in candy and other food products, but birds don't like methyl anthranilate, one of the components in Concord grapes. While the kiddies are happy chugging down the flavoring in a grape soda, birds won't go near the stuff, making it a safe, effective, tasty means of avian discouragement. ✳

There is another, less obvious example of forced perspective here. Stand in front of the fountain in the central courtyard. Notice how the **fountain and two successive planters** are wider at the front, with each of the three elements gradually narrowing and lengthening as they lead your eye to the back of the pavilion? This gives the illusion of a much longer walkway and adds to the feeling the Eiffel Tower really could be far away.

The small **maze-like garden** at the front of the pavilion is styled after those created by the famous French landscape artist André Le Nôtre. His stunning geometric designs can be seen at many famous chateaus and estates, including the Palace of Versailles.

Aux Vins de France offers samples of fine French wines, but there's a little secret here, too. Look up at the basket on the shelf behind the tasting counter. **Ratatouille**, the rat with culinary ambitions from the movie of the same name, is peeking out from among the grapes.

Even if you're not in the market for French perfume, you'll want to pop into the Librarie et Galerie. Head to the back of the shop and you'll find a lovely stained-glass window depicting scenes from the Beauty and the Beast fairytale. As you face the window, look to your left. On the top shelf you'll find the **magical rose in a glass bell jar** that shed its petals as the Beast waited to find true love. Belle has clearly found her prince, as the rose has all its petals again. Walk out the back door and around the corner to view the window from the outside.

While it makes for a convenient pathway from France to the United Kingdom Pavilion, the bridge you cross is based on the real-life pedestrian bridge **Pont des Arts**, which links the Louvre and Institut de France, crossing the river Seine. Don't forget to look over each side of the bridge as you go!

Imagine That!

Husband-and-wife Imagineers Steve and Kathy Kirk, senior vice president, creative executive and director, Creative Development, respectively, joined the team at WED Enterprises (the acronym for Walter Elias Disney, used prior to the department becoming WDI), in different ways, but their time with the company left a lasting impression on the parks, and on them. Steve was recruited by Disney Legend Rolly Crump in 1976 for his expertise in sculpture and artwork, beautifully represented in his creation of two of Epcot's most beloved characters, Figment and Dreamfinder, as well as the Dream Machine. Then he spent ten years creating the incredible

Tokyo DisneySea park. He says, "It is the story and character elements that make the charm. Technology helps deliver this story but is not the mainstay." Kathy came into WED in 1980, knowing nothing about the company, but feeling a job at Epcot "appeared fun." Her career took her to Tokyo Disneyland, where "documenting the various attractions and working with the Japanese culture to create a successful park" was her greatest thrill. Imagineers Kathy and Steve fondly recall their early days and the influence Walt still had on the Imagineering process. "When we started, Walt's hand-picked designers were still present, so his 'spirit,' so to speak, was still present, too. The designers and leaders were forever saying, 'Walt would. . . .'"

United Kingdom

British visitors may feel they have returned home when they reach the United Kingdom Pavilion. At least, they would if they lived at **Hampton Court**, the palace that inspired the building housing The Toy Soldier shop, across from the Rose & Crown Pub.

Again, no detail is too small when creating a real-life feel to a pavilion. When the pavilion was first built, it was deemed far too clean to be accurate. Painted-on **soot** was added to the chimneys to capture the essence of a typical British home, around the time of Mary Poppins and Bert the Chimney Sweep.

That post in the middle of the main walkway is a great photo spot and a terrific place to rest tired feet, but it is really a reproduction of a four-sided pillar **sundial**.

The lovely cottage housing The Tea Caddy shop is based on the Stratford-upon-Avon **cottage owned by Anne Hathaway**, wife of William Shakespeare. It was considered by Disney Imagineers to have the quintessential cottage look;

because thatching would not last long in Epcot, however, the roof is actually broom straw clipped to look like old thatching.

Citizens of medieval Britain were taxed on the ground floor square footage of their homes, so many buildings were built larger upstairs than downstairs. Notice the first floors of the shops on your left-hand side. This **overhang** also provided a shelter for pedestrians, who could walk under the cantilevered section, thus avoiding household waste thrown into the street from upstairs windows.

Before you pop into the Queen's Table, notice the **crests** in the shop's upstairs window. They represent Oxford, Eton, Edinburgh, and Cambridge, four of the United Kingdom's historic seats of learning.

Strolling around the back of the pavilion to the garden behind the shops, you will find a gazebo where British Invasion, a Beatles tribute band, plays. The building on your left as you face the gazebo represents the **1910 Edwardian style**, while the other side of the same building hints at **post-war London**. This dual use of building façades is a common technique used by Imagineers to make the most of the available space.

Enter the Toy Soldier and go all the way to the back of the store. There you'll find a library used by Mary Poppins (and, inexplicably, Winnie the Pooh). On the large coat and umbrella rack is a **bundle tied with string**, addressed to Mr. Banks, 17 Cherry Tree Lane, London. Fans of the story will recognize Mr. Banks as the father of Mary Poppins's young charges, Jane and Michael Banks.

To the right of the umbrella stand, you'll find a small grouping of photographs that clearly have meaning. They are pictures of **Christopher Robin Milne**, son of A. A. Milne, author of the charming *Winnie the Pooh* stories, holding his beloved bear. The photograph on the shelf above the grouping is of Milne and his son, to whom he told bear tales. Although Milne named the central human character in the *Winnie the Pooh* books after his son, the star of the story was not named after Christopher Robin's cuddly companion. His real-life stuffed bear was named Edward. Winnie the Pooh was named for a brown bear called Winnipeg—affectionately known as Winnie—who made her home at the London Zoo.

On the shelf below the photo grouping are **three envelopes**, one of which is addressed to Henry Pootle. It's hard to know who the recipient is, as it could be either Henry Pootle Press, publishers of the book, *A. A. Milne, a Handlist of His Writings for Children*, or for Pooh-bear's lovable little friend Piglet, jokingly referred to as an unrecognizable Henry Pootle after he'd been scrubbed clean in the bath.

A second letter is intended for Mr. Alexander Milne (A. A. Milne) and a third awaits delivery to a Mr. Sanders, 100 Acre Woods West. If you know your Pooh, you'll recognize Mr. Sanders as the name above Pooh's door, immortalized by the statement that Winnie the Pooh lived under (literally, in this case!) the name Sanders.

As you walk out of the pavilion, notice the three stained-glass windows to the left of the Crown and Crest sign, representing each of the three flags (England, Scotland, and Wales) that make up the Union Jack. Their mottos are **Tria juncta in uno** (Wales: *Three joined in one*, motto of the Order of the Bath); **Nemo me impone lacessit** (Scotland: *Nobody assails me with impunity*, motto of Scotland and the Order of the Thistle); and **Honi soit qui mal y pense** (England: *Evil be to him who evil thinks*, motto of the Order of the Garter).

> The Order of the Garter's origins are unclear, but a charming pos-
> sibility lies in the mishap of the countess of Salisbury, whose garter
> slipped from her leg while she was dancing in the company of King
> Edward. Unkind laughter on the part of various courtiers nearby
> prompted the king to utter the phrase, "Shamed be the person who
> thinks evil of it," that would inspire the order's motto. ✳

Rose and Crown's motto, posted above the doorway to the
restaurant, reads *Otium Cum Dignitate*. Translated it means
"Leisure with dignity," a mighty fine way to conduct oneself
through life. However, it may be worth noting at the time
the phrase was coined, those who were able to afford leisure
also associated the perk with another possible definition of the
word *dignity*, which is "worthiness." The upper classes were
considered worthy of leisure, with dignity or not.

Canada

Arriving at the final pavilion on our clockwise tour, two
distinct styles become obvious when you look closely. Eastern Canada is represented by the brick structures, while
wood was the building material of choice in western Canada.
The history of Canada, from the early European trappers to
the nineteenth-century Victorian influence, blends seamlessly, while the impressive Butchart-inspired sunken garden brings a grace and beauty to the otherwise rough terrain
of the Canadian Rocky Mountains.

The stand of **maple trees** in the garden represents Canada's
national symbol, the maple leaf. Why the maple leaf? Native
tribes passed on the importance of the tree's sap as a dietary
staple to European settlers arriving in Canada, and in the

1700s, the French-Canadian association, the Saint-Jean-Baptiste Society, adopted the leaf as its emblem. Later, English Canadians accepted the maple leaf as the national symbol.

To the right of the pathway leading down to Le Cellier restaurant is a **sunken garden** inspired by the efforts of Jennie Butchart, who reclaimed the limestone quarries dug up by her husband's company for the manufacture of cement on Vancouver Island. Rather than leave unsightly pits, Mrs. Butchart created glorious sunken gardens. They attract tens of thousands of guests who enjoy their beauty just as we enjoy the nod to her enterprising ways in the Canada Pavilion at Epcot.

You also find another example of forced perspective here. The plants near the bottom of the Rocky Mountains are much larger than those at the top. This gives the illusion of the mountain being higher than it really is.

Many of the native plants used in the landscaping do not thrive in the Florida heat. For ease in replacing those that wilt or die, the plants are not planted. They each sit in their own container and can be removed and replaced quickly.

Only one of the **totem poles** in the Canada Pavilion is real. Can you tell which one? (See Solution 6 in Appendix B for the answer.) The real totem pole was commissioned by Walt Disney Imagineering. WDI realized the error of their creative ways when they placed the totem pole crafted by a native artist next to the one Imagineering had already created and saw how cartoon-like theirs looked in comparison.

Canadian artist David Boxley's totem pole depicts a traditional **Raven story**, one of many told by the Tsimshian people as well as other Pacific Northwest indigenous peoples. Raven is a trickster whose antics often backfire, but everything somehow comes out right in the end, with a generous helping of insight into the customs of the Northwest natives' way of life. Here, Raven is forcing the Chief of the Skies to release the sun, the moon, and the stars.

Imagine That!

The Imagineering philosophy for EPCOT Center represented a real departure in the Disney theme park lineup. California's Disneyland and, later, Florida's Magic Kingdom focused on fun, with the occasional moral or semi-scholarly lesson thrown in. EPCOT Center was purpose-designed as the educational park, a risky decision that could have backfired. Walt Disney held the optimistic belief the park would be well received as long as guests were entertained as well as informed. Imagineer Marty Sklar fondly recalled Walt saying, "In our business you can educate people, but don't tell them you're doing it!"

Florida has a lot of things, but snow isn't one of them. To give the illusion of **snowcapped mountains** during the winter months, the Canada Pavilion's landscaping is replaced by all-white flowers and plants.

It would be tempting to sit on the **large rock** between the Canada Pavilion and the United Kingdom Pavilion for a perfect view of IllumiNations. However, the rock holds a secret. A section of the top opens up just prior to the show, allowing a 12-foot pole to emerge, with lights and speakers used during the show. Ouch—don't sit there!

Off Kilter, the must-see Celtic bagpipe rock band at the Canada Pavilion, actually has no Canadian members. The various musicians hail from Florida, Kentucky, Ireland, and, surprisingly enough, Puerto Rico. So what makes them appropriate to this pavilion? Not much, really. But notice the kilt worn by Jamie, the front-man playing the bagpipes. He wears the striking Nova Scotia tartan, which honors the Scottish influence in the founding of Canada's province of Nova Scotia

(Latin for New Scotland). Nova Scotia's Cape Breton Island is known for an energetic style of fiddling, brought over from Scotland, while the Scots and the Irish also introduced their native Celtic music to Canada. It's a bit of a stretch, but it works. Go see Off Kilter anyway. They're fabulous!

On your way out back into Future World, stop for another drink at the **fountain** near the children's splash fountains. Use the taller fountain and listen. It isn't always working, but when it is, what fun!

Epcot is full of special touches, but among the loveliest are the **twinkling sidewalks** between the Innoventions Plazas and Spaceship Earth. As you exit the park after IllumiNations, look down at the sidewalk just before you reach Spaceship Earth. They sparkle! If you take the route that passes Innoventions West, duck into the covered area near the door for an even more spectacular lighted sidewalk.

* Fascinating Fact

How does Epcot hire all those wonderful Cast Members in World Showcase? Through the Walt Disney World International Program or, more specifically, the Cultural Representative Program. Candidates must be eighteen years or older, from one of the represented countries, and have a good command of the English language. Once hired, they are paired up with roommates from countries different from their own, encouraging friendships to be forged in spite of cultural diversity. Many speak more than one language, but they are only allowed to work in their country's pavilion. *

And if you think you've seen everything just by touring the park, there's one more spectacle most people miss here at Epcot. As the crowds rush to the exit after IllumiNations ends, slow your pace and let World Showcase empty out. Now is the perfect time to stroll the walkway amid the peacefulness and the twinkling lights, and there is one final act that has to play out before Epcot is put to bed for the night. At some point between 10:00 and 10:30, the inferno barge out on World Showcase Lagoon undergoes a **fuel burn-off**, which, if you didn't know better, looks like the barge is exploding! It's an astonishing (but quick) sight and if you have the stamina to stick around for it, it's something you won't soon forget.

Discovery is Epcot's primary focus. Take the time to wander. You may just find that "one little spark" of imagination that inspired Epcot's opening-day theme, We've Just Begun to Dream!

Epcot Timeline

Walt Disney first described plans for EPCOT, the Experimental Prototype Community of Tomorrow, in October 1966, envisioning a working city where technology and creativity would combine, showcasing American ingenuity and the concept of free enterprise. His dream was never realized, because Walt passed away on December 15, 1966.

It wasn't until October 1, 1978, that Esmond Cardon "Card" Walker, president of Walt Disney Productions, formally announced plans to build what would become Walt Disney World's second theme park, rather than Walt's concept of a functioning community. Groundbreaking and construction of **EPCOT Center** began on October 1, 1979.

The park opened on October 1, 1982. During the opening-day ceremonies, Card Walker greeted guests with what is now a quintessential Disney slogan, "To all who enter this place of Joy, Hope, and Friendship—Welcome."

1982: Opening Attractions

The park opened with a series of special dedication ceremonies for the various attractions. The ceremonies took place during the first few weeks of the park's existence and highlighted each of the main attractions in turn.

Spaceship Earth was dedicated on October 1, 1982, followed by the **China** Pavilion on the third, **Universe of Energy** on the fourth, **World of Motion** on the fifth, **The Land** on the sixth, **The American Adventure** on the eleventh and twelfth, **Canada** on the thirteenth, **Italy** on the fourteenth, **Germany** on the fifteenth, **Communicore** on the eighteenth, **United Kingdom** on the nineteenth, and **France** and **Japan** on the twentieth.

The official **Grand Opening** took place October 22–24, 1982, with a dedication ceremony on the twenty-fourth. Representatives from around the world participated in a water-pouring ceremony, adding water from major rivers and seas around the world to the fountain in Innoventions Plaza. On October 23, EPCOT Center's first nighttime fireworks show, **Carnival de Lumier**, began.

On December 4, 1982, **Journey into Imagination** was dedicated, followed by **Mexico** on December 13.

1983–1988: A Period of IllumiNation

Horizons opened on October 1, 1983, with **A New World Fantasy** replacing Carnival de Lumier as the evening fireworks spectacle. On June 9, 1984, EPCOT Center hosted World Fest, featuring its first lagoon-based fireworks show, **Laserphonic Fantasy**. **Morocco** followed on September 7, 1984, the tenth pavilion in World Showcase.

Daytime show **Skyleidoscope** air and water pageant debuted in 1985, along with China's **Nine Dragons** and **Lotus Blossom Café** restaurants, but it would take until January 15, 1986, for another major attraction, **The Living Seas**, to open its doors, adding an eighth significant element to Future World.

The ground-breaking *Captain EO*, a blockbuster 3-D film produced by George Lucas, directed by Francis Coppola, and starring pop singer Michael Jackson, debuted on September 12, 1986, at the Magic Eye Theater, located in the same building as Journey into Imagination.

Two years later, on January 30, 1988, the breathtaking **IllumiNations** nighttime laser and fireworks show premiered, replacing Laserphonic Fantasy. Then, on May 6, 1988, World Showcase welcomed the **Norway** Pavilion, with the pavilion's ride, **Maelstrom**, opening four days later.

1989–1994: Wonders, Surprises, and Innoventions

On October 19, 1989, the **Wonders of Life** Pavilion opened in Future World, and Walt Disney World celebrated its twentieth anniversary a year later, an occasion honored at EPCOT Center by the arrival of **Surprise in the Skies** daytime show over the World Showcase Lagoon.

Another three years would pass before any major changes occurred, including an alteration to the park's name, as EPCOT Center officially became **Epcot '94**. On March 26, **Food Rocks** replaced Kitchen Kabaret at The Land Pavilion, while Communicore closed in January, returning as **Innoventions East and West** on July 1, and the very first **Flower and Garden Festival** was held—now one of the park's most successful annual events.

Next up was **Honey, I Shrunk the Audience**, a 3-D experience based on the hit movie *Honey, I Shrunk the Kids*, which arrived at the Magic Eye Theater on November 21, replacing *Captain EO*.

1995–1998: New Years, New Names

With the New Year came (another) new name, **Epcot '95**. Also new, on January 21, 1995, *The Circle of Life: An Environmental Fable* replaced *Symbiosis* at The Land Pavilion. The show featured characters from the blockbuster motion picture *The Lion King*; Disney movies had begun to play a role in Epcot's attractions. That summer, the first **Food and Wine Festival** debuted, another popular annual event which has gone on to become a major money-spinner.

Again, as the year changed so did the park's name, this time simply shortened (thankfully) to **Epcot**. World of Motion Pavilion closed on January 2, 1996, in preparation for a new attraction that would be so technologically advanced, its original projected opening date of summer 1997 was delayed for nearly two years as Imagineers worked out the bugs.

Ellen's Energy Adventure, starring popular television personalities Ellen DeGeneres and Bill Nye, replaced the original *Universe of Energy* show on September 15, 1996, adding a lighter touch to an attraction that was considered by some to be "too dry and factual."

1999–2000: Millennium Milestones

After a sixteen-year run, the Horizons Pavilion closed on January 9, 1999, and finally, on March 7, **Test Track** made its long-awaited debut in the former World of Motion Pavilion, racing its way into Epcot history as the attraction with the worst track record for breakdowns. However, the ride also became wildly popular, in contrast to **Journey into Your Imagination**, which effectively killed off beloved characters Dreamfinder and Figment when it replaced Journey into Imagination on October 1, 1999.

Unveiled on September 29, 1999, the massive **Mickey Wand** towered alongside Spaceship Earth, with its glittering Epcot 2000 signage. It would remain there for seven years, minus the 2000 portion once the Millennium Celebration ended.

The year-long celebration also scored a huge hit with the **Tapestry of Nations** parade and the specially revamped **IllumiNations: Reflections of Earth** laser and fireworks show, which debuted along with Journey into Your Imagination. Tapestry of Nations would be renamed **Tapestry of Dreams** in 2000, before ending its run in March 2003.

2001–2004: Figment Returns!

With a nod toward the public outcry caused by the original attraction's closure, **Journey into Imagination with Figment** replaced the 1999 version on June 1, 2002, and, happily, resurrected the little purple dragon.

Reflections of China replaced circle-vision Wonders of China on May 22, 2003, and another three months would pass before the state-of-the-art ride **Mission: SPACE** debuted on August 15, undergoing various adjustments over the course of the next few years as guests suffered motion sickness due to the realistic sensation of launching into space provided by the ride system's centrifuge.

Food Rocks at The Land Pavilion closed in January 2004, making room for a new attraction due the following year. At The Living Seas, the hugely imaginative **Turtle Talk with Crush** debuted in November 2004, adding more entertainment geared toward the six and under crowd, bringing another mega-hit movie character (from *Finding Nemo*) to Epcot—and creating far bigger crowds than anyone imagined!

2005–2006: The Land Has Liftoff

On May 5, 2005, Disneyland import **Soarin'** opened at The Land Pavilion, housed in a brand-new building branching off the main pavilion. A direct copy of Soarin' over California from Disney's California Adventure park, the attraction was an immediate success, with waiting time frequently topping 180 minutes.

Riding a tidal wave of popularity caused by Turtle Talk with Crush, The Living Seas underwent a much-needed refurbishment and emerged with a new name: **The Seas with Nemo and Friends**, in October 2006.

2007: Twenty-five Years to Celebrate

El Rio del Tiempo in the Mexico Pavilion went down for refurbishment and returned on April 6 as the **Gran Fiesta Tour Starring the Three Caballeros**. The park's icon, Spaceship Earth, also closed for a major overhaul shortly after its post-show area reopened after several years of dormancy as **The Project Tomorrow: Inventing the Wonders of the Future**.

In another long overdue move, the circle-vision film *O Canada!* returned on September 1, redone with comedian Martin Short as its onscreen host.

October 1, 2007, marked Epcot's twenty-fifth anniversary. Though no formal celebrations had been announced by Disney, a dedicated fan base organized a grass-roots acknowledgement of the milestone called **Celebration 25**. Epcot's vice president, Jim McPhee, announced a re-dedication ceremony would take place, highlighted by a second water-pouring ceremony and A Conversation With Marty Sklar, during which Disney legend Sklar spoke about the creation of the park, the challenges the Imagineers faced, and the impact Walt Disney's grand vision, realized in part through Epcot, has had upon the world.

Disney's Hollywood Studios

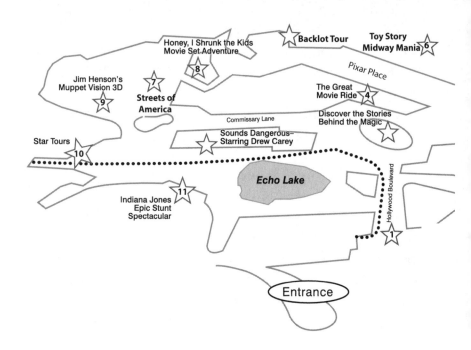

1. **Hollywood Boulevard:** See Mickey standing on top of Crossroads of the World kiosk? He has one ear higher than the other and his right hand is outstretched. What is he doing up there? His copper ear is grounded and acts as a lightning rod!

2. **Tower of Terror:** Just after you exit the library for your harrowing thirteen-story drop, notice the fuse boxes on the left-hand wall. Take a moment to give the handle a pull. You may get a rather shocking surprise!

3. **Rock 'n' Roller Coaster:** Check out the license plates as the limos pull up for takeoff. You might see UGOBABE, 1QKLIMO, H8TRFFC, and 2FAST4U.

4. **The Great Movie Ride:** This attraction offers two distinct scenarios, one with a cowboy theme, and the other with a gangster theme. If you have a preference, ask a Cast Member to direct you to the correct line.

5. **Animation Courtyard:** Want to sing in the rain with Gene Kelly? The street lamp on the corner has an umbrella attached. Stand on the black pad and pull the umbrella's handle for a delightful surprise.

6. **Toy Story Midway Mania:** Mr. Potato Head is the first Audio-Animatronic character that can remove and replace one of its own body parts.

Disney's Hollywood Studios

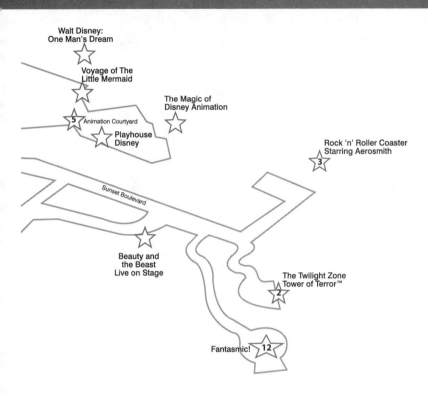

7. **Streets of America:** The red fire hydrant in the alley two blocks up from the San Francisco backdrop, next to the Chevrolet Building, opens at random, with a cooling (or possibly jolting) shower of water.

8. **Honey, I Shrunk the Kids Movie Set Adventure:** If you stick your hand inside the dog's nose, you might trigger a surprising reaction.

9. **Jim Henson's Muppet*Vision 3-D:** If you arrive before the pre-show movie starts, watch for the test pattern as Scooter crosses from one monitor to another. It's a hidden likeness of Kermit the Frog.

10. **Star Tours:** Pay attention to the various pages over the intercom while you're in the boarding area. You may hear a page for Egroeg Sacul (George Lucas spelled backward).

11. **Indiana Jones Epic Stunt Spectacular:** How does Indy avoid getting speared as he makes his way through the temple to retrieve the golden idol? He actually controls the release of the spears by stepping on square keypads, so he knows exactly when they will spring.

12. **Fantasmic!:** The riverboat ferrying the characters at the end of the show is a replica of the boat in Steamboat Willy. Notice who is up in the wheelhouse piloting the boat?

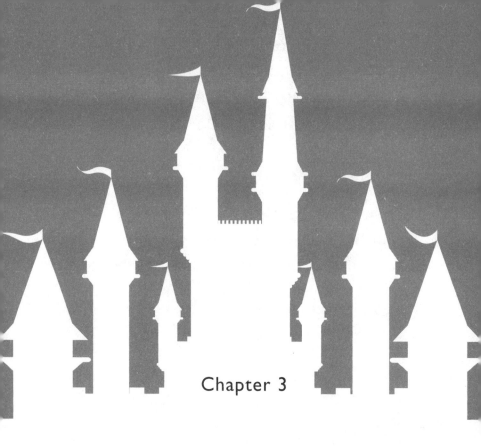

Chapter 3

Disney's Hollywood Studios

"**Welcome to the Hollywood** that never was and always will be," or so said Michael Eisner, chairman of Walt Disney World Company when Disney–MGM Studios opened in 1989. Enter the studios and you are placed firmly amid the glamour of Hollywood during its golden age, surrounded by sites, sounds, and characters that would have been familiar to the likes of Clark Gable, Rita Hayworth, Marilyn Monroe, and Richard Burton—the brightest stars of the 1930s, '40s and '50s.

Walk down any street in the park and you're likely to run across a starlet hoping to be discovered, a soon-to-be-famous director looking for extras for his blockbuster film, and public workers who just know their big break is right around the corner. On one side is a rendition of the theater where now-famous movies debuted, farther on you pass the restaurant where everyone who was anyone dined, hoping to see and be seen. While the original concept for the studios has been somewhat diluted over the years, the allure of being in that most glittering of towns, the tense excitement of a live movie set, and the pull you feel on your heartstrings when high drama is played out on stage and screen is not the stuff of make-believe; it's alive, vibrant, and immensely convincing. To be a star or to see the stars; the choice is yours!

Because Disney's Hollywood Studios (the name given to the park when Metro Goldwyn Mayer's licensing agreement ended in 2008) is based on a real time and place, much of what you experience is taken from real life. It is easy to recognize the movie, show, or stage play an attraction may be based upon, but the small touches that add up to an authentic atmosphere are often missed or taken for granted. If guests overlook certain aspects of the theme, the Imagineers have succeeded in creating a believable environment. But it would be a shame to miss all the little secrets they have placed around the park, some hidden and some not so hidden.

And now, the scene is set, you know your inspiration, and you have excellent direction. Ready? ACTION!

Hollywood Boulevard

One of the first elements greeting guests as they enter Disney's Hollywood Studios is the Crossroads of the World information kiosk, its spire rising high above Hollywood Boulevard.

The crossroads is a replica of the original Crossroads of the World in Hollywood, California, with the addition of Mickey Mouse standing proudly on top. Not only does the kiosk serve the functional purpose of providing park maps and various necessities to guests, it also serves a less obvious purpose. Mickey has one ear higher than the other and his right hand is outstretched. What is he doing up there? His copper ear is grounded and acts as a lightning rod!

The first shop on the left side as you enter the park is **Sid Cahuenga's One-of-a-Kind**. Sid's pays homage to the residents of Hollywood, nicknamed Cahuengas (pronounced "Co-enga") after the Treaty of Cahuenga, which ended the Mexican-American war in California. The name is derived from the village of Mocahuenga, located near a pass carved between Los Angeles and the San Fernando Valley, and Cahuengas were the final hold-outs who would not sell their homes when Hollywood was becoming commercialized. Sid's is the only place in Walt Disney World where you can buy an authentic photograph of Walt Disney. Sid's occasionally carries a signed version, which retails in the range of $3,000.

As you make your way down Hollywood Boulevard, you'll notice Magic Kingdom isn't the only park with a reason to peek in the windows. Remember to glance at the **upper-story windows** along Hollywood Boulevard and Sunset Boulevard to see who is advertising their services.

✳ Fascinating Fact

You have probably seen the roaring lion at the beginning of Metro-Goldwyn-Mayer (MGM) movies, but did you know the part of Leo the Lion has been played by several big cats? Since the movie studio's inception in 1924, five different felines—Slats, Jackie, Tanner, Brief Mane, and Leo the Lion—have preceded the opening credits. Leo's likeness could be seen on various icons and signage while the park was still called Disney–MGM Studios, but today no trace of him remains, other than on collectable Disney trading pins and in pre-2008 family photo albums. ✻

When you reach the junction of Hollywood Boulevard and Sunset Boulevard, stand in front of the Tip Board and look down at the half-oval plate in the pavement. It is marked **Est. 1928**, the year Mickey Mouse was first featured in the cartoon short, *Steamboat Willy*.

Now turn around and look behind you at the building across the road from the Tip Board. It has the 1928 reference, too, at the top of its rather bland façade. Most of the shops and facades in Hollywood Studios are based on real buildings, and this one takes its inspiration from the **Culver City Ivy Substation** in Culver City, California, a former train station that found its second life as a live-performance theater.

You will see **1928** on various buildings all over Hollywood Studios, so keep an eye out for them. To get you started, Hollywood & Vine restaurant across from Echo Lake is another location marked with Mickey's debut date. See how many more you can find!

Sunset Boulevard

Rather than joining the stampede of early-morning park-goers as they rush to Tower of Terror and Rock 'n' Roller Coaster, take the time to look at the area near the curb running alongside Sunset Boulevard. There are contractor's stamps at various points along the boulevard with the logo Mortimer Bros. Construction Co. 1928. Mortimer was the original name Walt Disney gave to the famous mouse, until his wife Lillian suggested Mickey was a friendlier name.

If you think Carthay Circle Theater gift shop, on the corner of Sunset Boulevard and Highland, just before the Theater of the Stars, *must* be a replica of something important, you would be right. It was inspired by the real **Carthay Circle Theater**, where Walt Disney's beloved *Snow White and the Seven Dwarfs*, the first full-length animated feature film, debuted. Had it not been for the success of that movie, Walt Disney's financial future would have been seriously in doubt, as he invested nearly everything he had toward production costs.

✳ Fascinating Fact

The original Carthay Circle Theater was located in Carthay, California, a residential district in Los Angeles, until it was torn down in 1970. Another famous film, <u>Gone with the Wind</u>, debuted there and it was one of only two theaters in the United States that featured Fantasound, the sound system pioneered by Walt Disney for the animated film, <u>Fantasia</u>. ✳

A bit farther down, the shop to the right of Villains in Vogue, with the intricate artwork at the top, is a nearly exact replica of the **35er**, the only bar in the Old Town area of Pasadena, California. Disney decided to go one better by making the detailing at the top a striking green, in keeping with the art nouveau style, while the original building was left unpainted.

As you make your way toward the end of the street, pause to look at the red trolley parked in front of Sunset Market

Ranch. The trolley has a clever hidden date on the front and the side. Sunset Boulevard opened on June 2, 1994. This opening date is commemorated as the trolley's number, **694**. Just a few weeks later, on July 22, 1994, the screams coming from the Tower of Terror would begin.

Notice those patches of red brick with **trolley track** showing through the pavement along Sunset Boulevard, just before you reach Tower of Terror and Rock 'n' Roller Coaster? An area provisionally called Tinseltown Street was slated to open along Sunset Boulevard in the early 1990s with a Toontown Trolley ride, Baby Herman's Runaway Buggy Ride, and Benny the Cab ride. Unfortunately, Tinseltown Street never made it past the concept stages. All that is left of the brilliant idea is trolley tracks, paved over and going nowhere.

Tower of Terror

When you reach the end of Sunset Boulevard, you can't help but notice Hollywood Studios' most easily recognized attraction. Tower of Terror is a massive edifice filled with secrets, some fascinating, some just downright creepy.

One hidden gem can be found straight away. Immediately after you enter the lobby, look at the wall directly to the right of the concierge desk. The Hollywood Tower Hotel has been awarded the AAA (American Automobile Association) **13-Diamond award**, but AAA's real rating system only goes up to five diamonds. It's just a little nudge toward the superstitious and the beginnings of an inescapable sense of foreboding.

As you walk through the lobby, notice the **pair of glasses** on the concierge table in the lobby. If you look closely, you will see their lenses are broken. In the *Twilight Zone* television show's episode, "Time Enough at Last," Henry Bemis finally has the time to read the books he loves because he is the lone survivor of a nuclear attack. Just as he gathers his books around him, his glasses fall from the table and the lenses shatter, leaving him nearly blind and unable to pursue his selfish pastime. Sometimes the glasses here mysteriously move into the library, so look for them there if you do not find them in the lobby.

Imagine That!

Eric Jacobson, then producer–art director for the Twilight Zone Tower of Terror, talks about the decisions faced by WDI when creating an attraction based on a popular cultural icon. "We really had a challenge trying to figure out what the Fifth Dimension scene should be. That's the part of the ride where the elevator car goes horizontally through space. No one had ever realized what the Fifth Dimension was in the Twilight Zone, they had just talked about it. We took a lot of the elements of the opening of the show and some of the specific story points that we had created for our ride, and mixed them up. We found another art director to help us realize what the mission should be, then we probably did four or five full scale mockups of that scene. Each time we said, 'No that's not right,' until we got to the final one and said, 'Ok, now we've got it. That's what we're going to do.'"

One of the creepiest secrets in the tower will require you to step out of the queue briefly, so bear in mind you may have a few other guests (who are not "in the know" as you are!) pass you as you take a quick look. See that **bulletin board**, just to the left of the queue in the small hallway before you enter the library? A series of letters have fallen away from the main text and have mysteriously formed themselves into a warning to the hotel guests. Even spookier, they have a way of returning to their correct locations, so this secret is sometimes visible, sometimes not. If they are not on the bottom of the sign during your visit, check Solution 7 in Appendix B to find out which words the dropped letters are supposed to spell out.

Once inside the library, where Rod Serling tells you the story of the tower (some of it in his own voice, which was painstakingly pieced together, in part from the *Twilight Zone* episode "It's a Good Life"), you may recognize props representing various show episodes. Above the bookcase next to the TV in the library you'll see the **demonic popup device** from "The Nick of Time" episode; the **metal robot** from "The Invaders" sits on the ledge above you; an **envelope** with the name Mary on the front from the episode "A World of His Own"; and the book from the "To Serve Man" episode (during which the townspeople were horrified to discover the alien's benevolent-looking book was actually a cookbook!), rests on a table opposite and diagonal to the television monitor.

There are other *Twilight Zone* references here, too. The **trumpet** sitting on top of a page of sheet music in the library recalls the episode titled "A Passage for Trumpet," in which Joey Crown, convinced he will never amount to anything, throws himself in front of a truck after selling his beloved trumpet to a pawn shop. He ends up in limbo and has to make a decision between life and death.

During the pre-show movie, Rod Serling informs you that Hollywood's elite have taken refuge from the storm for the night, among them a child star and her governess. Notice the cuddly stuffed toy she is holding when she enters the elevator. It's an **original Mickey Mouse** plush; curiously enough, it currently sells for more than $500 on eBay.

When the pre-show ends, allow other guests to exit the
library ahead of you so that you can walk through the rest of
the queue at a slower pace. Just after you exit the library for
your harrowing thirteen-story drop, notice the **fuse boxes** on
the left-hand wall. Take a moment to give the handle a pull.
You may (or may not, depending on whether they are in full
working order) get a rather shocking surprise! Don't worry;
it won't hurt, so even the kiddies can give it a try.

✳ Fascinating Fact

Because it would ruin the illusion to have airplane beacons on top
of the Tower of Terror, the structure is only 199 feet tall, a foot short of
the 200-foot height at which beacons would be required. Cinderella
Castle at Magic Kingdom and the Tree of Life at Animal Kingdom
have also avoided the need for beacons, but Epcot's Spaceship
Earth was not so lucky. ✳

Just after you enter the ride elevator, look for the **safety
inspection certificate** signed by Mr. Cadwallader, indicating the elevator is in good working order. The certificate is
dated October 31, 1939, the day the Tower Hotel opened
(and, of course, a spooky reference to Halloween night). The
certificate commemorates an episode of *Twilight Zone* titled
"Escape Clause," in which Cadwallader, the devil in disguise,
grants immortality to Walter Bedeker in exchange for his
soul should he later choose not to live. The inspection certificate is number 10259, the numeric version of October 2,
1959, and refers to the date the first *Twilight Zone* episode
aired. Now that you know the elevator has passed inspection,
take your seat and venture into the terrifying unknown!

Once you come to your senses again after your hair-raising journey, look for the poster in the exit lobby advertising the **Anthony Freemont Orchestra** playing at the Tip Top Club. The Tip Top Club is the restaurant at the top of the hotel where the doomed guests you saw in the pre-show movie were heading for dinner when lightning struck.

Speaking of the top of the hotel, do you remember seeing the tower sticking up from behind the Morocco Pavilion when viewed from the Mexico Pavilion in Epcot? While you are here, be sure to notice how the architectural elements at the back of the tower look somewhat Moroccan in style. If you look closely, they don't appear quite the same from the front as they do from the back. It's all a matter of what your eye expects to see.

If you are very lucky, you may meet up with one of the bellhops (Cast Members) at the tower who has been "checking in guests" since the tower opened. If you see a bellhop with **gold epaulets**, you've found an original TOT Cast Member. A nice touch and a neat badge of honor, don't you think?

Rock 'n' Roller Coaster

Just around the bend lies another chance to scream for all you're worth. Rock 'n' Roller Coaster represents a bit of a departure from Disney's usual family-friendly style, and it brought more teen-appeal to the park when the ride opened in 1999.

Winding your way through the queue, before you reach Studio C where you will meet Aerosmith for your invitation to hop aboard the stretch limo that takes you to the concert, stop when you reach Studios A and B and listen. You can hear the band during their **recording sessions** as they were laying down the tracks played over the speakers in your limo. You will also hear various names being paged over the intercom as you work your way toward the sound stage; they are the names of the Imagineers instrumental in creating the attraction.

Concert posters line the walls, adding to the atmosphere as you queue, but some aspects of concert culture are not considered appropriate for a family theme park. The placement of the smaller American flag on the MC5 poster is a bit odd, given that it is not originally part of the poster but instead has been placed there to cover up a **marijuana leaf**. If you look closely you will see it through the flag.

✳ Fascinating Fact

Wonder what you are in for when you board your stretch limo? Get ready for a zero-to-sixty launch in only 2.8 seconds, nearly five Gs of force (the space shuttle only reaches three Gs at liftoff!), a corkscrew, two roll-over loops, and Aerosmith blaring in your ear courtesy of five speakers . . . per passenger! WOW!! ✳

Do you need something to do to take your mind off the launch at the beginning of Rock 'n' Roller Coaster as you approach the boarding area? Check out the **license plates** as the limos pull up for takeoff. You might see UGOBABE, 1QKLIMO, H8TRFFC, and 2FAST4U. Get it? If not, read them as if they were words.

That intercom you heard before you reached Studio C is still trying to track people down. If you listen for one name in particular as you approach the boarding area, you may hear someone on the intercom say, "Phone call for Jude on line one. Hey, Jude! Pick up line one!" It is, of course, a clever reference to the Beatles song, "**Hey Jude**."

You're almost to the loading area and although you may not know what to expect from the ride, there is no doubt about what is expected of you! Take a look at the blue guitar-shaped sign giving safety instructions for guests while riding. There is a humorous notation at the bottom, "**Thank you vera much**," a subtle nod to Elvis Presley and his slight variation on the use of the English language.

Those **safety harnesses** you will be clutching for dear life aren't there to keep you in the limo as it speeds along the track. Centrifugal force will hold you in your seat even without the harness. They are there to keep you locked in your seat in case the attraction must make an emergency stop. Notice you didn't have to place your belongings in a locker? In case of an emergency, you will stay in the car but that bag holding your brand-new Goofy hat might end up on the floor.

Imagine That!

Walt Disney's spirit is very much alive in how WDI operates, even today. Imagineer Eddie Sotto, with WDI from 1986 to 1999, explains, "You're there to take everything further and push the envelope. That was Walt. The public expects you to take what could only be in a movie and make it real. Quite a challenge. So you have to have an attitude that allows you to be flexible as to all kinds of ways of achieving the fantasy for the guest. So it takes Walt's risk-taking process to get there, and some courage. I was told once, 'never underestimate someone who overestimates themselves.' When I stopped laughing it hit me: If you're not aware that you're incapable of something, then it's more likely you'll make it happen!"

Courtyard

Returning to this park's version of a central hub, the courtyard area is home to Hollywood's Brown Derby restaurant which, in its original incarnation, played host to the best and the brightest during Tinsel Town's heyday. Hollywood Studios' version also pays tribute to the stars whose portraits covered the walls of the landmark restaurant. The portraits in black frames are laser copies of originals; those in gold actually are the authentic portraits. Although the California-based restaurant no longer exists, it has been faithfully recreated here, looking just as it would have looked in 1946, with one exception: this Brown Derby has tables to accommodate a large number of guests while the California version only had booths, allowing for more privacy.

Before you enter the main dining area, take a look at the **guest book** in the entry area. It has signatures of all the stars who have eaten in Hollywood Studios' Brown Derby. Browse through it as you wait for your table (or pop in for a quick peek if you're not dining there today).

Each of the parks has a reference to its **opening day**, and you may be wondering where Disney–MGM Studios' (using the park's original name) opening day is commemorated. Walk back to the central courtyard and look for the large bronze statue of a producer with a movie camera. Before the statue arrived, there was a plaque here that honored the park's debut; sadly, it is no longer on display. Once it was clear Metro-Goldwyn-Mayer's partnership with Disney would end, the plaque was removed. While the statue certainly makes a great photo opportunity, it's a shame not to have a memorial of the grand premiere.

Tinker Bell, one of Disney's most beloved characters, nearly became a footnote in animation history. Margaret Kerry remembers, "After Peter Pan, Tinker Bell was not going to do anything else. Then Walt Disney decided to make this theme park in a place called Anaheim. The consensus of opinion was, 'God help us! Anaheim? Walt's going to lose his shirt.' Roy Disney was asked to tell Walt not to use any of the licensed characters that were generating most of the company's money, because if any of these characters were involved with a project that failed, they were going to be worthless. Walt thought about it and said, 'I'm going to use Jiminy Cricket and Tinker Bell in the park. Will that satisfy them?' and that's the reason those two characters came back to life."

Farther along, acting as the park's original central icon (although the Sorcerer's Hat certainly takes away from the effect and is now meant to be the official park icon), Mann's Chinese Theater probably looks familiar to many guests. It is a replica of the Hollywood landmark, **Grauman's Chinese Theater**, which opened in 1927. Sid Grauman, original owner of Grauman's Chinese Theater in California, came up with the idea of casting stars' footprints in cement, starting with Mary Pickford, Norma Talmadge, and Douglas Fairbanks. He also created the idea of the ultraglamorous Hollywood movie premiere.

As you enter the theater's front courtyard, look down. Many visiting celebrities have left their **signatures and handprints** in cement squares. See if you can find George Lucas, Dick Van Dyke, Roger Rabbit, C-3PO, and others. You may even find the distinct prints of Mickey Mouse and Minnie Mouse!

But don't stop looking yet. Look for actor Charlton Heston's signature. Or I should say, "**Charton Heston**." It seems Mr. Heston was interrupted as he was signing his name; when his focus returned to his work, he'd accidentally skipped the letter *l* in his first name. Hence, he is forever immortalized in cement as Charton Heston.

Take a moment to find one more signature square. Leonard Nimoy, the actor who played Mr. Spock in the popular 1966–1969 television show, *Star Trek*, placed his hands in the Vulcan "**live long and prosper**" formation. Remember that hand sign, because you're going to see it again when you ride Toy Story Midway Mania. (Don't worry, though, I'll remind you when you reach the right spot.)

The Great Movie Ride

The Great Movie Ride is your chance to ride the movies; a grand spectacle waits on the other side of the marquee. But first, take the time to inspect each of the props as you queue through the lobby. There are many cinematic treasures here, including the **carousel horse** from *Mary Poppins*, an authentic prop used in the film. Other props in the queue are original, too, but they are displayed on a rotating basis so they may be different each time you visit.

Once the director shouts, "Action!" the real Technicolor journey begins. The attraction's first scene, a five-tiered cake supporting starlets in shiny swimwear, is a faithful replica of a scene entitled "By a Waterfall," choreographed by Busby Berkeley in the 1933 film extravaganza, *Footlight Parade*. The ride originally included an active fountain of water, just as the movie's bathing beauty scene does, but sadly, that feature went the way of the Swan Boats and Captain Nemo's

Nautilus over at Magic Kingdom. Expensive to maintain, cost won out over style.

The Great Movie Ride offers two distinct scenarios, one with a cowboy theme, and the other with a gangster theme, so if you have a preference, ask a Cast Member to direct you to the correct line. If you opt for the gangster version, notice the **license plate number** on the car in the shootout scene. It's 021-429, a variation on February 14, 1929, the date of the infamous St. Valentine's Day Massacre in Chicago.

✳ Fascinating Fact

The Emmy Award takes its name from a feminization of the word immy, a slang term for the image orthicon tubes used during the early days of television, prior to the 1960s. Emmy was deemed more feminine, in keeping with the statue's lovely lady in gold. We indirectly owe the name Emmy to President Dwight D. Eisenhower. The award was originally intended to be named for the iconoscope tube, nicknamed the "Ike," which was also President Eisenhower's nickname. To avoid confusion, Immy, then Emmy, won out. ✳

As soon as you enter the James Cagney scene just after the *Mary Poppins* setting, look at the posters on the wall to your left. The bottom of one of them has been torn, and you can see **Mickey Mouse's shoes** peeking out from behind. You may also notice **shadows** passing by the window of the Patrick J. Ryan building as you enter the same scene.

Keep looking to your left as you pass through the gangster scene. You may catch a glimpse of **Mickey's silhouette** in the right-hand corner of the Western Chemical Company building's upper window.

In the cowboy version of the ride, you may wonder if Wyatt Earp will come strolling out of the scenery, and your expectation wouldn't be unreasonable. The town you travel through certainly recalls Tombstone, Arizona, "The town too tough to die." **Cochise County Court House** (indicative of the county where Tombstone is actually located) is on your right, covered in Wells Fargo posters offering rewards for the Most Wanted outlaws. The *Tombstone Epitaph* is on your left, a recreation of the real-life *Tombstone Epitaph*, which carried the story of the gunfight at the O.K. Corral in the October 27, 1881, edition. Curiously enough, the University of Arizona's Department of Journalism still publishes a paper under that name, with the tag-line "No Tombstone Is Complete Without Its Epitaph."

If you look to the right in the same scene, on the Cochise County Court House building, just past Clint Eastwood, you'll see a sign advertising **Ransom Stoddard**, Attorney. Senator Ransom Stoddard was a character played by Jimmy Stewart in the 1962 John Wayne movie, *The Man Who Shot Liberty Valance.*

Guests with an exceptionally quick eye may notice some of the hieroglyphics on the walls in the Egyptian scene have rather surprising icons. See if you can locate **R2-D2 and C-3PO** from the *Star Wars* movie (look directly across from Indiana Jones, on the left-hand side of the tram, just about at eye level near the snakes). You will have to look quickly, so you may want to seek this one out on a second ride-through.

A large hieroglyph featuring Donald Duck as an Egyptian servant offering a slice of cheese to **Pharaoh Mickey Mouse** can be found on the left-hand wall in the Well of Souls scene, directly in the corner of the third tier of hieroglyphs, just before you leave the area. Again, look quickly!

If you are sitting on the left side of the tram as you pass through the *Indiana Jones* scene, beware some of the **snakes** on the shelves. They move! But don't worry; they don't jump, so you're safe . . . for the moment.

If you are sitting on the extreme left side of the tram, you may be able to read the computer monitors if you peer over the edge of your vehicle as you travel through the *Alien* scene. The screen titled **Crew Status Roster** shows a listing of the Imagineers and designers of The Great Movie Ride. Notice each crew member's current status; some are listed as missing while others have humorous notations next to their names.

How does a director let viewers know the brave scouting crew rooting around in an empty alien craft are in for some serious trouble? Cue the **alien slime!** The drippy bits that fall on your tram (and you) are just drops of water on the Great Movie Ride. But the slime dripping down the sides of the scene are a mixture of water and glycol for that super-creepy, ultramessy effect.

* Fascinating Fact

Want to make a batch of alien slime at home? It's as simple as mixing enough water and glycol (available at any pharmacy) to create a pleasing, slimy consistency. Don't want the kiddies to get it all over the couch? Try this recipe instead: Dissolve five teaspoons borax in one cup water. Add mixture to one-half cup white glue, one teaspoon at a time. Stir, adding more borax as needed to get a semi-firm but slippery consistency. Add food coloring if desired, rinse well to remove stickiness, and you've got kid-friendly slime. *

You may recall having seen the rear half of a **Lockheed Electra 12A airplane** as you made your way around the Jungle

Cruise at Magic Kingdom, and you certainly can't miss the front half, which features prominently in the *Casablanca* scene. It isn't the original plane used in the movie, however. The Lockheed Electra 12A in the movie was actually a mockup, not a real airplane.

You will be able to see Munchkin Land shortly before you enter the first *Wizard of Oz* scene. Notice how the Yellow Brick Road forms itself into the letter *O* at the beginning, and then trails off toward the second scene. When you reach the scene with Dorothy and her friends, look at the Yellow Brick Road as it ends in front of the Emerald City. Notice how it forms the letter **Z**, effectively tying both scenes to the word *Oz*.

Pay particular attention to the **Wicked Witch** when she makes her dramatic appearance shortly after your tram stops. Prior to the A-100 technology used in making the witch, Audio-Animatronics could not move quickly without looking unnatural, giving her the distinction of being the first to exhibit more natural movements. As amazing as this technology is, it still takes an entire week to program fifteen seconds of motion.

Imagine That!

Many attractions are so beautifully presented that it is difficult to single out the smaller details. But they are no less important, as Eric Jacobson, senior vice president, Creative, at WDI attests. "I was producer–art director on the Great Movie Ride, and our team researched all those movies that we included in the ride, over and over again. We read books and watched them on video. Back in the 1980s the equipment that we had to work with wasn't as sophisticated as it is now, but we printed out black-and white-frames from a lot of the movies so that we could really slow it down and look to see, for example, exactly what the Wicked Witch of the West's costumes looked like. We noticed as we looked at the film in slow frame-by-frame, that she actually has a purse around her waist that, probably, nobody has really noticed. So we said, that's a neat detail we want to include to make sure her costume is as authentic as it could possibly be, even though it would be very simple to eliminate something like that because most people probably won't even notice it in the attraction."

Animation Courtyard

Animation Courtyard originally debuted as the working heart of Disney's Hollywood Studios, a place where guests could watch Disney artists as they went about their craft, take a tram ride past a division of the wardrobe and construction departments, and get a sense of the true behind-the-scenes operations that bring the movies to life.

Walt Disney: One Man's Dream

Walt Disney: One Man's Dream isn't a secret, but it contains so many wonderful pieces of memorabilia it would be a shame to miss it. Pay particular attention to the **school desk** from Walt's early years, when that naughty boy carved his initials into the top of the desk. Apparently, education wasn't at the top of his favorite attractions list, either; Walt only attended one year of high school.

You might not have time to snap a quick family photo before your group departs for the **Backlot Tour**, so the attraction designers have thoughtfully placed a photo-op tram near the entry to the attraction. But watch out . . . you may get misted!

If the tram's mist didn't cool you down, Coca-Cola should do the trick. Stand in front of the **giant Coke bottle**, but be sure you hand someone your camera first.

Who can forget Gene Kelly singing in the rain in the 1952 movie of the same name? If you ever had the wistful desire to dance in a downpour, you will have your chance when you reach the intersection directly across from Lights, Motors, Action! just to the right of the San Francisco backdrop. The street lamp on the corner has an **umbrella** attached. Stand on the black pad and hold on to pull the umbrella's handle for a delightful surprise and a terrific picture for the family photo album.

Pixar Studios

Along with the 2008 launch of the park's new name, Pixar Studios found a permanent place in Walt Disney World, solidifying the Disney-Pixar merger in high style with the opening of Toy Story Midway Mania. As Disney's newest attraction, the attention to detail is outstanding, and you'll find lots of hidden gems here in the land "where toys come to work and play."

You will recall many of the buildings in Disney's Hollywood Studios are based on real structures, and in the case of Pixar Studios, that couldn't be truer. The large gateway you pass through is a replica of Pixar's gateway in Emeryville, California, and the **bricks** used throughout the area were chosen to exactly match those at the Emeryville animation studio.

Toy Story Midway Mania marked two firsts for Walt Disney Imagineering: the simultaneous creation of a ride that would premiere at both Walt Disney World and Disneyland in California, and a curious design quirk that required Imagineers to don 3-D glasses when working with the blacklight paint, to make sure they were doing it correctly!

Once you pass under the Pixar gateway, walk over to the small building on your right. Andy has taped his crayon drawing of a **Command Post** setup on the window of the building's doorway. Now turn around and look at the rooftops of the buildings on your left. He has set up his green army men, Scrabble game pieces, and Tinkertoys according to his hand-drawn diagram.

Toy Story Midway Mania

As soon as you pass by the pale blue **Crayola crayon** just before you enter the attraction, you get a sense of having shrunk to the size of a toy. Once you reach the boarding area, you have symbolically entered Andy's room and you're interacting with his toys. They've discovered a new midway game under the bed.

Before you enter the line, take a quick look at the elaborate toy-inspired sign above the doorway. Do you notice anything odd about it? Probably not. However, although the title above the door is **Toy Story Midway Mania**, the Florida version was originally called Toy Story Mania—and that is the name used by Imagineers on press releases and on some merchandise—while the California version simply used the nondescript title, Midway Mania. California's version was then renamed Toy Story Midway Mania, which gave it the necessary tie to the movie, and ultimately, they both officially took on the Toy Story Midway Mania title. Almost makes your brain hurt, doesn't it?

Shortly after you enter the attraction you will come across the first of Andy's assortment of books, with more scattered throughout the queue and the boarding area. Most of them are books that were **influential childhood reading**, such as *The Boy Scout Handbook*, *Babes in Toyland*, and *The Little Reader's*

Collection of Children's Stories, or **Pixar short films**, such as *Red's Dream* and *Knick Knack*. You will also see many of the same books if you pay close attention to Andy's bookshelf in the *Toy Story* movie. However, there are a few exceptions. On your right-hand side shortly after you enter the queue are *Frogs: Where Did They All Go?* by Tom Carlisle and *Magic Made Easy* by J. Ranft. Tom Carlisle is Pixar's Animation Studios facilities director and J. Ranft memorializes Joseph Ranft, Disney and Pixar storyboard supervisor before his death in 2005. Ranft was nominated for an Academy Award for Best Writing, Screenplay Written Directly for the Screen, for his work on the *Toy Story* movie. Just across from the boarding area a stack of books painted on the wall includes the book *Smyrl Smyrl Twist and Twirl*, which refers to Eliot Smyrl, a member of Pixar's modeling and animation systems development team that worked on the first *Toy Story* movie.

As you make your slow, winding way toward the loading area you will pass by many of Andy's Lincoln Log creations. Some of them give the distinct impression that Andy may have been a budding Imagineer. Like most children, he doesn't necessarily have the engineering part of the equation exactly right, but he did come up with a creative solution. Those blobs of blue and pink you see at the corners of some of the structures are meant to be **Play-Doh** and **Silly Putty**, used as a quick fix to keep Andy's constructions upright.

You will also notice Andy is a prolific artist, as evidenced by all of his drawings throughout the queue, and the crayons scattered around. Look at the **points of the crayons** as you walk past. Some have been used extensively, while others haven't been used at all.

A delightful bit of Imagineering whimsy comes in the form of a balsawood airplane, along the right-hand side of the queue. While most people are familiar with the inexpensive childhood toy, this one has a rather special name. It's a **Blue Sky** flyer, in reference to Imagineering's Blue Sky Studio and the process of brainstorming—called the "blue sky" phase—used by Imagineers when creating new concepts for shows and attractions.

Imagine That!

When designing new attractions, the Imagineers take their inspiration from many places. Chrissie Allen, senior show producer, recalls the initial process for Toy Story Midway Mania, "We were really inspired by the Buzz Lightyear ride. How can we make it more competitive and more repeatable? You may notice every time you stop at a game, the vehicle records your score along with your percentage. That's the kind of technology we love nowadays. It's an invisible technology, guests have no idea how we're doing it, and that's what we like to achieve. It is a combination of these things and the combination of a lot of exciting technologies wrapped in a new way. A lot of this is still old technology. It's a bar ride (meaning, the ride vehicles are linked together by a bar) that has spin turrets, and they have been around for many years. But we've added computer technology, gaming technology, and the latest projection techniques, and that's what takes us to a new level."

Acting as a carnival game barker, **Mr. Potato Head** certainly grabs your attention as you walk through the queue, but that's not the only thing he can grab. The technology used to create him is so advanced, he holds the distinction of being the first Audio-Animatronic character that can remove and replace one of its own body parts. He's also the first to have a mouth that looks like it forms real words as he is speaking and eyes that look directly at individual guests.

Some of Andy's handiwork can be found on the wall just after you turn the corner past Mr. Potato Head, but before you pick up your 3-D glasses. Andy has painted some of his favorite characters, and if you are a **Hidden Mickey** fan, take a look toward the bottom of the finger-painting where you see Nemo from *Finding Nemo*. Just below him, you'll see the famous tri-circle Mickey silhouette.

Once you reach the boarding area, you have entered Andy's room and you are now, symbolically, one of his toys. Everything looks giant-sized, including the **Christmas lights** strung along the top of the central Tinkertoy structure. True to life, one of the bulbs—the blue bulb directly above the loading area—is burned out.

Just before you enter the game itself, you will see the Toy Story Midway Games Play Set on the right-hand wall, with a bar code on the bottom left side. There are several numbers around the bar code, as you would expect, but the number on the bottom left of the bar code is the **number 121506**. That number refers to the date Toy Story Midway Mania was officially announced as Hollywood Studios' newest attraction in the making.

There is a hidden bit of technical magic to Toy Story Mania that guests will never see and certainly won't be thinking about it as they take aim at the various midway targets. A zealous devotion to accuracy went into creating the attraction so that riders would experience a sense of realistic, seamless game play. The Imagineers required each game to be created in real life; then the technology used in making the on-screen games believable was based on the way the real games played. When you shoot at a target or toss a ring, your ammunition flies and lands exactly as it would if you were physically playing the game.

Your focus will be firmly on the game after you board your ride vehicle and set off for some midway mania, but once you have launched your final dart at Woody's Rootin' Tootin' Shootin' Roundup and Buzz Lightyear tallies up your score, notice the split-fingered **hand gesture** he makes as he says goodbye. It's the Vulcan "live long and prosper" sign, which you also saw in Leonard Nimoy's cement handprints at the Great Movie Ride.

Imagine That!

Appealing to young and old alike was a primary goal for the Imagineers during the design process for Toy Story Midway Mania. Senior show producer for the attraction, Sue Bryan, says, "When you look at how broad our audience is, we really wanted to make this attraction appeal to everybody and also make everyone feel like they were successful and had a good time. It's no fun to play a game and feel like, 'Oh, I don't play games and I'm not going to do well.' We started play-testing and we had very simple software mockups to try to find out what's fun for everybody and how could we make different levels of challenge so that a three-year-old who can't aim, a teenager who plays games all the time, and my father who has never played a game in his life can literally get into the carnival tram, pull the string, and be successful from the start. So if you look at the scenes, the different sizes of targets, the different movements of the target you can see we spent an unbelievable amount of time tuning that and testing with people. It's really a passion for us to make sure that everybody got off smiling and feeling like they did a good job."

Although you will be happily chattering away about your score and how quickly you can get through the queue again for a second ride, there is one final touch that will

pull gently at the heartstrings of anyone over the age of
forty. Just before you leave the unloading area, you will
pass by an enormous Little Golden Book, open so that you
can see the front and back covers. Like many of the toys
and games found throughout the queue and in Andy's
room, Little Golden Books played a significant literary
role in many Americans' early childhood. Since the first
title, *The Poky Little Puppy*, debuted in 1942, more than
two billion Little Golden Books have been sold, and it's
a safe bet to say, they all eventually had **tattered corners**
from being so well loved, just as the one here in Andy's
room does.

Before you leave the Pixar Studios area on your way to
Streets of America, look at the poster advertising Toy Story
Midway Mania, hanging from a light fixture to your right.
The poster's frame is made from used **Popsicle sticks**, stained
so you can tell which flavor each of them was!

Streets of America

The hustle-bustle found in any big city in America has been
beautifully captured along Streets of America, both in terms
of the architecture and the ambient sounds. As you walk
along the street, you can hear streetcars, police whistles,
noisy buses, and the hurried sounds of daily life. A wonderful touch, don't you think?

During the worst heat of summer, big cities such as
New York and Chicago provide welcome relief from blister-
ing temperatures by opening up the fire hydrants in many
neighborhoods, creating a perfect water fountain for over-
heated residents to run through. The red **fire hydrant** in the

alley two blocks up from the San Francisco backdrop, next to the Chevrolet Building, opens at random, with a cooling (or possibly jolting) shower of water that children and children-at-heart can't resist.

Looking down the alley intersecting Streets of America, to the left of *Honey, I Shrunk the Kids* Movie Set Adventure, you can't help but notice the backdrop of San Francisco, just the ticket if you want to convince friends you also visited California during your vacation. A newsstand on the left side of the backdrop is also worth exploring. Notice the **newspaper headlines**, in particular the headline on the *San Francisco Times*. There's no promotion like self-promotion and Steamboat Willie has made the front cover! On the right-hand side of the backdrop are two **newspaper boxes**. By now, you know it's worth taking a quick look.

Honey, I Shrunk the Kids Movie Set Adventure

If you have children in your group, you're likely to spend some time exploring the *Honey, I Shrunk the Kids* Movie Set Adventure, a larger-than-life playground filled with all things climbing, jumping, and sliding. Even if you don't have children with you, stop in for some terrific photo opportunities; a favorite is the giant dog. With his face so close to the ground, it's a given you'll want to stick your hand inside the **dog's nose**. Go ahead . . . try it! You may trigger a surprising reaction.

After your visit to the play area, return to the San Francisco backdrop and turn left. New York is just a few steps away, and you'll know you've reached it when you see the New York Public Library on your left. Just across from the library is the entry to the Eighteenth Street Station, servicing subway lines **W** and **D**. Although New York's real yellow line W is the Broadway Local line and line D eventually reaches Broadway, they are not part of the same route. Line D is the orange Sixth Avenue Express. More likely, this version is a nod in the direction of Walt Disney's initials. If you look down the stairwell, you'll see the version here is also a dead-end. That part is accurate, since the original Eighteenth Street Station closed in 1948 and is no longer accessible from the street.

At the end of the same block, just before you turn the corner toward the home of the Muppets, pause for a moment and look through the window to the left of the first set of doors for **Venture Travel Service**. Although the travel agency is obviously an advertisement for your next Walt Disney World or Disney Cruise Line vacation, there's a treasure here, too. The picture hanging on the left-hand wall features Walt and Lillian Disney, with Walt holding an original plush Mickey Mouse.

Imagine That!

Theme is paramount when it comes to creating an attraction or a show, but it isn't the only element Imagineers keep in mind as they come up with design concepts. Imagineer Sue Bryan explains, "Part of what we're trying to do is give families a reason to talk to each other, to give them a topic as they leave. Not just that they had fun here, but to have a discussion they'll continue as they leave. Particularly with the little kids, the excitement is so pure."

Meals at Mama Melrose's are a "masterpiece in pasta" and that love of the arts continues on the back wall of the building where Mama advertises her cooking. In the courtyard just past Al's Toy Barn as you are heading toward

Jim Henson's Muppet*Vision 3-D, you'll find a quirky rendition of another famous masterpiece. **Mona Lisa** has become a California girl, smiling behind her shades, with her *I *heart* L.A.* pin and the Hollywood sign in the background.

Jim Henson's Muppet*Vision 3-D

As you approach Muppet*Vision (from the Star Tours side), you will see a long wall topped with planters full of flowers. However, one of the planters isn't filled with a bouquet. Instead it's an **ice cream sundae**. And if you look at the planter at the far end, you'll see that someone already ate the sundae contained in that planter, leaving nothing but the spoon.

Time flies when you're in Walt Disney World but **Gonzo** has taken the idea just a bit too far. Look up at the clock on the front of Muppet*Vision. That's him, hanging from the minute hand.

Just after you enter the Muppet*Vision building, there is a box office to your right. The ticket seller has gone out, but he left a note saying the **key is under the mat**. You know you want to, so go ahead and lift the mat.

There are two bulletin boards on the left-hand wall after you pass through the turnstiles. One is the **Muppet*Vision 3D World Headquarters Directory** and the other is **The Rest of the Directory**. Take a moment to look at some of the humorous names and departments listed on each.

---

* Fascinating Fact

Jim Henson's Muppet*Vision 3-D is the only show on Disney property where the glasses are actually called 3-D glasses. They are Safety Goggles at Epcot's Honey, I Shrunk the Audience and Bug Eyes at Animal Kingdom's It's Tough to Be a Bug. *

If you arrive before the pre-show movie starts, watch for the test pattern as Scooter crosses from one monitor to another. It's a hidden likeness of **Kermit the Frog**.

Muppet*Vision's pre-show holding area is filled with jokes, some of them obvious, some less so. Just after you enter the room, look up at the net filled with red and green squares of Jello. It's a pun on the name of Mickey's famous Mouseke-teer, Annette Funicello. Get it? **A net full of Jello**.

Now look for the flattened fruit at the front of the pre-show area. They are a play on the words *Tutti Fruity* (**2-D Fruities**). Try not to groan too loudly.

Hanging toward the front left-hand side of the pre-show area, you'll see a poster of a Muppet that looks oddly familiar. It is a fitting memorial to the Muppets creator, **Jim Henson**, Muppetized, and with a movie camera lens around his neck.

Don't look now, but some of those **soldiers** standing on the rafters above you in the pre-show area aren't wearing pants. And, horrors! They haven't found them by the time they reach the final scene in the 3-D movie, either!

Once you enter the theater, you can't miss the penguins in the orchestra pit; they are obviously not paying attention to the **sheet music** in front of them. It's actually the score to "The Rainbow Connection," written by Kenny Ascher and Paul Williams, and sung by Kermit the Frog in the opening number of *A Muppet Movie*.

Although they've no doubt seen it several million times by now, the **penguins** do pay close attention to the show. Keep an eye on them and you may see them interact with the characters on screen. For example, when Bean Bunny flutters the bumblebee in front of Miss Piggy during her "Dream a Little Dream" solo, one of the penguins stands up and plays a rousing rendition of "Flight of the Bumblebee."

Let ordinary theaters show their movies on Bell and Howell projectors. The Muppets prefer to use their own brand, like the projector at the back of the Muppet*Vision theater, made especially for them by **Yell and Howl**. A close look at the projector also reveals two familiar faces. A ball on top of the projector is wearing glasses, making it look a lot like **Dr. Bunsen Honeydew**, while the whistle's bulging eyes are a close approximation of his assistant, **Beaker**.

If you are among the last guests to exit the Muppet*Vision theater, take a look at the walls and the projector area where the Swedish Chef fired off his cannon. You can watch the theater re-set itself for the next show.

Star Tours

If you have seen the *Star Wars* movies, you're already aware the Star Tours attraction is going to be seriously high-energy. As you are queuing toward the boarding area, pay attention to the various pages over the intercom and you may hear a page for **Egroeg Sacul** (George Lucas spelled backward) or **Tom Morrow**, which you might recall is a tribute to an Imagineer who worked on the now-extinct Mission to Mars at Magic Kingdom. Tom Morrow can also be found in robotic form at Epcot's Innovations West. He was originally cast as an Audio-Animatronic operational director for Flight to the Moon at Disneyland and later received a mention in the introductory video at Magic Kingdom's defunct Alien Encounter. He certainly gets around!

Another important announcement may grab your attention while you are queuing, especially if you did not heed the advice to make a note of where you parked when you arrived today. Listen for an announcement asking the owner of a speeder whose license plate has the number **THX 1138**, and would they please remove it from the no-hover zone. *THX 1138* was the first movie made by George Lucas in 1971, an adaptation of a short film he created while at the University of Southern California.

As you enter the room with the moving baskets along the Star Tours queue, look over the railing at the bits and pieces lying around. See if you can find the **robotic Kermit the Frog** sitting on the edge of one of the shelves below you and to the left of G2-9T, who is working on another robot. Then watch the **foot** connected to the pair of trousers lying to the left of Kermit. It moves!

In the second room you enter as you are queuing, take a look at the **boxes** passing by overhead. The letters and numbers on them are the initials and birthdates of the Imagineers who designed and created the attraction, another silent but not quite hidden set of signatures.

✳ Fascinating Fact

The Star Speeder 3000 you enter as you board Star Tours is the same motion-simulator technology used by the United States military to train their pilots. ✳

Once you board the ride vehicle, all manner of madness breaks loose. You're on an unexpected journey into the unknown with an inexperienced driver at the helm, and anything could happen! Captain Rex, your unwitting Star Speeder pilot, quickly assesses the situation just before he flies into the ice crystal and then delivers the classic line, "**I've got a bad feeling about this**." The quote is a recurring statement throughout the *Star Wars* series and entirely appropriate at this point in your adventure. Hold on tight!

Poor Captain Rex never had a chance. Once you're back on terra firma and the lights come back on, take a look at the red tag dangling from his processor. It reads, **Remove Before Flight**. After a trip like that, you may be wondering if his processor *was* removed, or if some smart engineer thought Rex himself should have been banished!

✱ Fascinating Fact

Think you'll have a more thrilling ride if you leave your seat belt unbuckled on Star Tours? The ride designers made sure that won't happen. Although it looks like the Cast Member monitoring the Star Speeder is pushing buttons to set the ride in motion when they open the small door on the left side of the Speeder, they are actually checking to see that all the LED lights on the panel are green, meaning everyone has buckled their seat belt. If a light corresponding to an occupied seat isn't green, no one gets a ride until everyone is secure and the lights are lit. Safety first, you know! ✱

Even those guests who suffer from motion discomfort or a physical ailment that won't allow a comfortable ride on Star Tours may be able to enjoy the attraction without the sensation of motion, though this little bit of hidden magic is not something Cast Members offer without prompting. Wait until the attraction no longer has a wait time, and then ask a Cast Member if you can ride when they perform a **flight check**, which is the process of cycling the show without the simulator going into motion.

It isn't a secret, but many guests don't realize they can sit on the **Imperial Speeder** bike prop across from Star Tours. If you align your camera just right and really ham it up, the resulting picture will be a fairly convincing shot from the speeder chase in the forest scene on Endor in *Return of the Jedi*.

If you pass by Star Tours in the evening when the area is quiet and you listen closely, you may hear **Ewoks** talking, chanting, and drumming. But remember, they only come out after sunset (or around 7:00 during those late sunset months). You can hear them best near the building's entry and at the far end of the forest, an area that normally is unused unless lines are extremely long. Walk back there during slower times when you can stop and listen for a while.

Be sure to look up at the treetops as you are listening for the Ewoks and you'll notice their little huts light up with **nighttime fires**. It's a delightful piece of hidden magic that most guests miss, and a peaceful retreat as your day winds down.

Backlot Express

Even if you have already eaten lunch or dinner, make your way over to the Backlot Express restaurant between Star Tours and Indiana Jones Stunt Spectacular. The small seating area to the left of the food counter, all the way in the back, holds a real back lot gem. Eddie Valliant's famous ride in the **Toontown taxi** was built around the frame you see over in the corner. Look at the bulletin board behind the car frame to see before and after photos.

On your way to the Toontown Taxi frame, you passed under a **yellow submarine** hanging from the ceiling. No, it isn't in honor of the famous Beatles song, but it *is* from the famous (and now extinct) Magic Kingdom attraction, 20,000 Leagues Under the Sea. The submarine was part of the background scenery you saw on your trip around the lagoon.

✳ Fascinating Fact

Although the popular submarine ride at Magic Kingdom is well and truly sunk, Disney Company didn't give up on the attraction altogether. Guests can still explore the watery depths with Captain Nemo at Disneyland Paris and Tokyo DisneySea. Sadly, but appropriately, Disneyland California's version has been taken over by another Nemo, of Finding Nemo fame. ✳

Are you ready for something a bit spooky on your way out of the Backlot Express? Exit through the doors on the right leading out to the upper seating area (as opposed to those exiting into the courtyard where the police car from *Roger Rabbit* is displayed). Before you exit, look at the plaster casts on the shelf above the windows. While each one is interesting in its own right, the **cast of the nun** (second from the left) is particularly curious. So curious, in fact, that she notices everyone who enters and exits. Watch her eyes as you pass by; she is watching you!

Indiana Jones Epic Stunt Spectacular

High thrills are in store at Indiana Jones Stunt Spectacular, where the stunts are real and so is the danger. How does Indy avoid getting speared as he makes his way through the temple to retrieve the golden idol? He actually controls the release of the spears by stepping on **square keypads**, so he knows exactly when they will spring. But yes, they are real and he could get hurt.

After Indy's heart-pounding escape from being crushed by the **giant boulder**, it's always a good laugh to see the stage hands roll the ball back to its starting position. It doesn't look heavy when they move it but, in fact, it's made from 400 pounds of rubber.

Fans of the *Indiana Jones* series will remember George Lucas wrote or co-wrote all of the *Star Wars* movies as well as the *Indiana Jones* films. In an obvious nod to his creative genius, the two series are tied together here at the Epic Stunt Spectacular when Indy delivers the line, "I've got a bad feeling about this," just before the fight with the masked acrobats in the Cairo scene. You will certainly recall the harrowing moment when Captain Rex said it during your ride on Star Tours!

With everything going on aboveground, it's easy to miss what's going on beneath your feet. As you pass by the entry to Indiana Jones Stunt Spectacular, to the left of the entry, down the path on the right-hand side, there is a well with a sign saying, **Do NOT pull the rope**. Notice *NOT* has been crossed out. You know what to do by now!

Imagine That!

How do Imagineers know when they've created a sure-fire hit? The best attraction, says Rilous Carter, vice president, Hollywood Studios, "is one that is conducive to every single person in the family. So whether you're fifty-seven, sixty, seventy years old, if you have kids three, four, five years old, they can ride with their parents and they can participate. I think that alone drives repeat visitation. You find when people get off an attraction, the kids want to get right back on it."

Most guests walk right by the short pathway between the Indiana Jones theater and the Indiana Jones Adventure Outpost, but it's worth taking a quick look. **Movie props** such as a World War I tank and an army truck can be found in the landscaping, while the roof of the Adventure Outpost harbors a cleverly disguised sniper's outlook.

Commissary Lane

Enormous piles of food served in the shadow of hokey B-movies while you sit in your convertible (or in this case, conver-table) under the night sky make a meal at Sci-Fi Dine-In Theater worth seeking out. If you can tear your eyes from the screen in front of you, notice the letters and numbers on each car's license plate. They are the initials and birthdates of the restaurant's designers and Imagineers. California, New Mexico, and Arizona are the only states represented on the license plates at Sci Fi Diner and are, not-so-coincidentally, the three states with the most UFO sightings in America.

Echo Lake

Located around a small lake, just as the tiny town of Echo Lake, California, is set around its namesake body of water, this charming area of Hollywood Studios has several opportunities for a snack or a meal, and some lovely hidden magic.

Sounds Dangerous—Starring Drew Carey

It's no secret Sounds Dangerous—Starring Drew Carey is all about making noise. But many guests rush right through the post-show lobby and miss several fun interactive opportunities to make some noise of their own. Even fewer guests realize the doors lining the back wall lead to sound booths and a short auditory experience. Although you may choose not to take the time to hear it all, look at the **props** along the upper wall. Each of them was used to provide sound effects in various Disney movies. Who knew you could use the glass from a hurricane lamp to make growling animal sounds?

With the overload of atmosphere, it is easy to overlook some of the more obvious details. Very few guests pay much attention to the **courtyard of busts**, just to the right of Sounds Dangerous, which provides lots of good photo opportunities and is a terrific viewing location for the afternoon parade. Walt Disney, Bill Cosby, and Marlene Dietrich are among those innovative thinkers honored here, with their likenesses and a description of their contributions to the world of entertainment.

Min and Bill's Dockside Diner, situated right on the lagoon, is more than just a relaxing spot for a quick snack, it's also a tribute to the 1930 movie, *Min and Bill*, in which actress Marie Dressler plays dockside innkeeper Min Divot and Wallace Beery is Bill, her fisherman boyfriend. Dressler won an Academy Award for Best Actress for her portrayal of Min, who struggles tirelessly to spare her adoptive daughter the worst the world has to offer.

As if Min and Bill weren't busy enough, their dockside location is also a worldwide shipping port. An inspection of the crates sitting on the dock to the front-left of the diner reveals **Max Bialystock** (from the movie *The Producers*) is eagerly awaiting a delivery from the Anita Doubleset Ledger Co., **Charles Foster Cane** (*Citizen Kane*) has placed an order with the Rosebud Sled Co., and **Rick's American Café** (made famous in the movie *Casablanca*) will soon be restocking supplies compliments of Quartz Wine & Spirits LTD.

Just across the lagoon, Gertie the Dinosaur is more than just a quick snack stop during your Hollywood Studios visit, she is also a tribute to **Windsor Mackay**, a vaudevillian actor who created Gertie as an addition to his show. She was the first projected cartoon (and an inspiration for Walt Disney's future works) in the days before multiplane cameras. It took over 14,400 drawings, done on rice paper, to create the desired effect and give the illusion Gertie was interacting with Mr. Mackay.

✳ Fascinating Fact

Gertie the Dinosaur is an example of the architectural style known as California Crazy. Southern California in the 1920s and '30s flourished with many such roadside curiosities designed to capture the attention of the traveling public as they sped along the highway at a dizzying 35 miles per hour. A giant puppy housing a hot dog stand, bakeries shaped like windmills, massive mushrooms, larger–than-life flowerpots and elephants, even the Great Sphinx of Egypt were a sure-fire way of attracting patrons into an establishment for a meal, a fill-up of gasoline, or a mortgage on a new home. ✳

Eddie Valliant, Private Investigator advertises his service on the window above the Hollywood & Vine restaurant, to the right of Gertie and just across the pavement. Although he insists on "No Toons," if you look closely you may notice **Roger Rabbit** isn't far away.

Before you leave Echo Lake, take a quick peek at the **Cosmetic Dentistry** building, just around the bend from Hollywood & Vine restaurant and across from the Dockside Diner. There is a directory on the right-hand wall next to the door that advertises for C. Howie Pullum DDS, Ruth Canal DDS, and Les Payne DDS.

The building next to Cosmetic Dentistry has a **For Rent** sign in the upper window, which isn't particularly compelling on its own, but as with all things Imagineering, it was placed there for a reason. When Walt and Roy Disney were just starting out, their initial base was in an uncle's garage until they amassed enough money to rent their own studio space. They finally found a location they could afford, right above the Holly-Vermont Realty company, whose logo you will see on the door below the For Rent sign. A nice tribute to a humble start, don't you think?

Hollywood Hills Amphitheater

Purpose-built for Hollywood Studios' nighttime entertainment offering, the amphitheater plays to sell-out crowds every night, in peak seasons.

Fantasmic!

Hollywood Studios' nighttime spectacular, *Fantasmic!* showcases Mickey's struggle against the Disney villains, all with a happy ending and the chance to see many of the Disney movie characters. The riverboat ferrying the characters at the end of the show is a replica of the boat in *Steamboat Willy*. Notice who is up in the wheelhouse piloting the boat?

Fantasmic! is canceled more often than any other show in Orlando. Why? Consider the following: The large mountain rising up from the stage is made of metal, there are 1.9 million gallons of water in the moat surrounding the stage, the bench-style seats guests sit on are made of metal, and Florida is the "Lightning Capital of the World."

And with that, it's a wrap!

Disney's Hollywood Studios Timeline

In April 1985, the Walt Disney Company announced plans to build a third gate at Orlando's Walt Disney World Resort. The $300 million park would be based on "The Hollywood that never was—and always will be." On May 1, 1989, Disney–MGM Studios welcomed its first guests, offering just five attractions, two theaters, one exhibit, a walking tour, a handful of "streetmosphere" actors, eight restaurants, and four shopping outlets.

The attractions open on May 1 were the **Great Movie Ride, Backstage Studio Tour, Superstar Television,** the **Monster Sound Show,** and the **Magic of Disney Animation** with the film *Back to Neverland.* Also open was the **Behind the Scenes Special Effects** walking tour, **SoundWorks** exhibit, and **Theater of the Stars** featuring *Now Playing.* Shortly after the grand opening, on August 25, the *Indiana Jones Epic Stunt Spectacular* held its first performance, with audience members playing bit parts in the show.

On August 24, the excitement surrounding the **Star Tours** attraction, due to open at the end of 1989, cranked up a notch as the **Ewok Village** opened at the future attraction's entrance. Then, on December 15, the ride itself, based on the massively popular *Star Wars* films, blasted directly into thrill-ride mega-hit fame.

1990: Muppets, Turtles, & Fireworks

The Broadway-style live musical *Dick Tracy Starring in Diamond Double-Cross* premiered in the Theater of the Stars on May 21, 1990, followed a day later by another new show, *Here Come the Muppets*, a stage performance with Kermit and Friends designed to generate interest in the Muppet attraction due to open the next year.

Five- to twelve-year-old boys everywhere were ecstatic when the **Teenage Mutant Ninja Turtles**, whose street show and meet-and-greet opportunities drew enormous crowds, arrived at MGM Studios. Youngsters were also the target market for the *Honey, I Shrunk the Kids* **Movie Set Adventure** (based on the 1989 movie, *Honey, I Shrunk the Kids* starring comedian Rick Moranis) which opened on December 17, 1990.

But the brightest addition in 1990 was the visually spectacular **Sorcery in the Sky** nightly fireworks finale, an awe-inspiring pyrotechnics display with The Chinese Theater in the foreground.

1991–1992: Frogs and Princesses

On February 16, 1991, less than a year after its first performance, *Dick Tracy Starring in Diamond Double-Cross* closed. It would be replaced by *Hollywood's Pretty Woman* show on September 24.

In May 1991, *Jim Henson's Muppet*Vision 3-D* began serving up in-your-face laughs, both on screen and throughout the theater. The *Here Come the Muppets* show closed in early September to make way for a new attraction, but, having formally acquired the rights to use Muppet characters in the Disney parks after Muppet creator Jim Henson's death in 1990, MGM Studios unveiled the

Muppets on Location: Days of Swine & Roses street show and meet-and-greet on September 16. Shortly after, characters from the television show Dinosaur took over traveling stages originally intended for the Muppets when the **Dinosaurs Live** parade rolled in on September 26. Beginning on November 22, 1991, *Beauty and the Beast—Live on Stage* dazzled guests, young and old, as the characters from the movie of the same name were brought to life in the Theater of the Stars. The princess craze had begun.

Voyage of the Little Mermaid, a live musical extravaganza, started 1992 off on the right foot. Ariel and a host of puppet characters sang and danced their way through scenes from the 1989 blockbuster movie, *The Little Mermaid*, while, out in the streets of MGM Studios, the year ended on another high note as the characters from cinematic smash hit *Aladdin* marched along the parade route in **Aladdin's Royal Caravan Parade**, debuting in December.

1993–1995: Towering Achievements

Things were quiet indeed as MGM Studios ran on autopilot through 1993. In honor of television's greatest actors, the **ATAS** (Academy of Television Arts and Sciences) **Hall of Fame Plaza** was unveiled, featuring busts of beloved entertainment icons from the 1930s to the present day. However, on the other side of the park the noise level was about to ratchet up by several decibels. Ground broke on May 28 for a massive new thrill ride, due to open in little more than a year.

Every park has a stampede attraction, and on July 22, 1994, Disney–MGM Studios opened the gates and the mad dash to the end of Sunset Boulevard began! **The** *Twilight*

Zone **Tower of Terror** officially opened its doors and the enthusiastic screams have not stopped since. It would be another five years before the park welcomed a new attraction, but for now, the tower offered plenty to keep the thrill-ride fanatics happy.

In 1995, the Backlot Theater played host to *The Spirit of Pocahontas* stage show, which opened in support of the big-screen movie, *Pocahontas.* On November 22, heroes from the blockbuster movie *Toy Story* began marching down Hollywood Boulevard in the new **Toy Story Parade**, replacing the lovable Aladdin and his friends. Over the years, guests had been asking for more character encounters, and Disney responded. Meeting beloved animated favorites had become an integral part of the theme park experience.

But the shining jewel in the 1995 crown had to be the premier of the **Osborne Spectacle of Lights**, a dazzling nighttime presentation shown only during the Christmas season. Buildings along Residential Street were decorated with elaborate light displays, along with dancing vignettes, sculptures, vast archways, and seasonal slogans, all made with millions of multicolored lights.

1996–1997: The Quiet Years

Disney–MGM Studios coasted along with a few relatively minor changes from 1996 to 1998 as funds and attention were focused on creating Disney's fourth gate, **Disney's Animal Kingdom**. *The Spirit of Pocahontas* show was replaced in 1996 by *The Hunchback of Notre Dame: A Musical Adventure*, another live musical featuring characters, some in the form of puppets, from the movie *Hunchback of Notre Dame.*

After a two-year run, the Toy Story Parade was replaced by another movie-inspired offering, the **Hercules "Zero to Hero" Victory Parade** in December 1997 and, in response to the popularity of R. L. Stein's best-selling book series, *Goosebumps*, the *Goosebumps* **Horrorland Fright Show** brought the book's scary central characters to life along New York Street in a fiendish street show young boys seemed to love.

Later that year, The Osborne Spectacle of Lights was expanded and renamed the **Spectacle of Lights with the Osborne Family Light Display**, and was by that time a huge Disney fan favourite.

Hercules and friends marched in their final parade performance in May 1998. On June 19, **Disney's Mulan Parade** arrived, with brand new characters from the feature film *Mulan*, which premiered in movie theaters on the same day.

1998–1999: Fantastic? No, Fantasmic!

Sorcery in the Sky was no longer showing as of 1998, and the need for a new evening show was of pressing importance. On October 15, *Fantasmic!* premiered, a character fest starring Mickey Mouse as he battled the forces of good and evil, and the show immediately drew record nighttime crowds. The 6,900-seat, purpose-built Hollywood Hills Amphitheater filled up nightly to standing-room-only crowds (to a total capacity of 9,900). *Fantasmic!* gave the park a huge boost in the form of much-needed evening entertainment.

The unusual audio-adventure, ***Sounds Dangerous Starring Drew Carey***, replaced the original *Monster Sound Show*, plunging visitors into darkness while Detective Carey bungled his way through a crime scene.

A year later, on July 29, **Rock 'n' Roller Coaster Starring Aerosmith** debuted, bringing the Hollywood Studios firmly into the realm of theme park status. It was an odd fit, having nothing to do with Hollywood, the big screen, or the little screen, but it was welcomed enthusiastically nonetheless.

The park's youngest guests, most of whom would not make the new attraction's four-foot height requirement, were not forgotten. In February 1999, television characters Doug, Skeeter, and Patti Mayonnaise from the show *Doug* delighted young guests with a new stage show, *Disney's Doug Live!*

In August, a second stage show—spun off from the beloved children's television show of the same name—*Bear in the Big Blue House* worked its gentle magic, heralding a new emphasis that would permeate the parks over the coming years. Preschoolers and attractions that appealed to them were now very much on Disney's radar.

MGM Studios was a far cry from its humble beginnings. It now truly had something for everyone.

2000–2001: TV Takeover

The park remained quiet in 2000, but, in April 2001, television's über-hit *Who Wants to Be a Millionaire* spawned the theme-park equivalent in **Who Wants to Be a Millionaire—Play It!** The new attraction proved to be so addictive, at one point there were restrictions on how many times per day each guest could be a contestant. With a grand prize of a three-night Disney Cruise (with airfare!), the repeat factor was enormous. However, most hot-seat winners walked away with a pin or a hat.

On October 1, 2001, Walt Disney World also launched its **100 Years of Magic** celebration. MGM Studios honored its founder with a new attraction, **Walt Disney: One Man's Dream**, featuring exhibits, artifacts and a lovely ten-minute film showing the highlights of the great visionary's life.

The same day, *Bear in the Big Blue House* became *Playhouse Disney—Live on Stage* (starring Bear, with his television friends from Rolie Polie Olie, Stanley, and the Book of Pooh). The show would have several character changes over the years; JoJo's Circus replaced Rolie Polie Olie in March 2005, and Mickey Mouse Clubhouse, Handy Manny, and Little Einstein joined JoJo and Friends in January 2008.

The Mulan parade ended in March 2001 and was replaced on October 1 by a more general offering, the **Stars and Motorcars Parade**, featuring favorite Disney movie characters along with classic characters, some riding in appropriately themed cars. Mr. M. Mouse and company were in attendance, and even the *Star Wars* characters got in on the action!

2003–2007: High-Octane Thrills

The following two years 2003 through 2004 were fairly quiet, though Residential Street underwent an extensive rerouting in 2003 to make way for a Disneyland Resort Paris import called *Moteurs . . . Action! Stunt Show Spectacular*. On May 5, 2005, *Lights, Motors, Action! Extreme Stunt Show* roared into MGM Studios, adding dynamic, high-octane energy to the far left corner of the park. Real movie-making had come to life!

C. S. Lewis' classic *Chronicles of Narnia* stories were made into a feature film, *The Chronicles of Narnia: The Lion, the Witch, and the Wardrobe*, in 2005. It would go on to win eleven Academy Awards and a place in MGM Studios. On December 9, 2005, **Journey into Narnia: Creating the Lion, the Witch, and the Wardrobe** opened in an empty soundstage on Mickey Avenue, a veritable winter-wonderland of artifacts and costumes from the movie, storyboards and walk-through exhibits, accessed though massive red doors resembling the famous fictional wardrobe.

Aimed at the pre-teen crowd, **High School Musical Pep Rally**, originally ill-placed in Magic Kingdom, found a new home as a mobile street show-cum-parade at MGM Studios on January 21, 2007. The East Side High Wildcats whipped the crowds into a frenzy of pep-rally cheering. The show has since been revamped and renamed **High School Musical 3: Senior Year–Right Here!**, with less "you can be anything" preachiness, more song and dance, and a big high school helping of audience participation.

2008: A Whole New Name

On August 9, 2007, the president of Walt Disney World, Meg Crofton, announced an impending name change at the Studios, emphasizing the park's new focus on a broader range of entertainment. Then, on January 7, 2008, Disney–MGM Studios formally became **Disney's Hollywood Studios.**

In recognition of the merger between Disney and Pixar Studios, Stars and Motorcars parade was replaced on March 14 by the high-energy **Block Party Bash Parade**, featuring a host of Pixar characters dancing and playing their way along the parade route, with a maximum of guest interaction.

Then, on May 30, the ambitious **Toy Story Midway Mania** attraction debuted, placing a firm punctuation mark on the park's dedication to family entertainment, and guests of all ages were truly delighted. The Journey Into Narnia walk-through exhibit was transformed into **Journey Into Narnia: Prince Caspian** in June, and featured props from the second movie. In February 2009 **The American Idol Experience** debuted, bringing the popular television show to the Studios, adding even more live, hands-on appeal to the energetic Hollywood experience.

Disney's Animal Kingdom

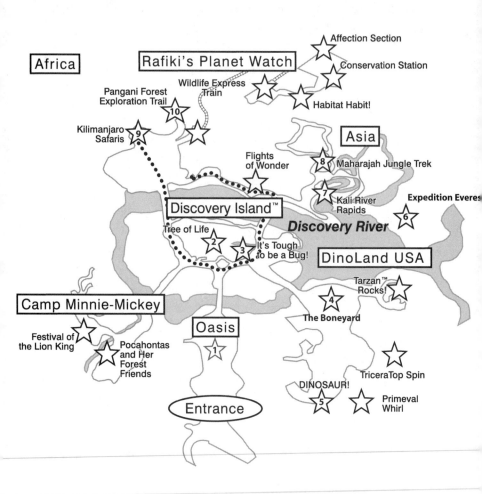

Africa

Rafiki's Planet Watch

Affection Section

Conservation Station

Wildlife Express Train

Habitat Habit!

Pangani Forest Exploration Trail

Kilimanjaro Safaris

Asia

Maharajah Jungle Trek

Flights of Wonder

Kali River Rapids

Expedition Everest

Discovery Island™

Tree of Life

Discovery River

It's Tough to be a Bug!

DinoLand USA

Tarzan™ Rocks!

Camp Minnie-Mickey

The Boneyard

Festival of the Lion King

Pocahontas and Her Forest Friends

Oasis

TriceraTop Spin

DINOSAUR!

Primeval Whirl

Entrance

Disney's Animal Kingdom

1. **Oasis:** All of the benches in Disney's Animal Kingdom are made of recycled milk jugs.

2. **Tree of Life:** There are 325 reptiles, mammals, and birds carved into the Tree of Life.

3. **It's Tough to Be a Bug:** The animatronics version of Hopper is eight feet tall and is one of the most complex ever made.

4. **The Boneyard:** Step on the footprints embedded in the ground and you may hear a growl, a trumpet, or a roar erupt from the caves behind you.

5. **Dinosaur!:** If you aren't too frightened about your impending trip back in time, pay attention to the name of the scientist who is about to send you on your search-and-recovery mission. His name is Dr. Grant Seeker.

6. **Expedition Everest:** See all that firewood on the rooftops? It isn't used for heating or cooking. Wood is scarce high up in the mountains so having a stack of it on your rooftop is an indication of wealth.

The more wood you have, the wealthier you are.

7. **Kali River Rapids:** As you wait in line, you will be able to hear loggers cutting trees in the distance, an indication of what's to come on your journey down the rapids.

8. **Maharajah Jungle Trek:** Look for the hidden Mickeys in the mural of the maharajahs along the wall running through the Jungle Trek.

9. **Kilimanjaro Safaris:** Environmental protection is of the utmost importance at Animal Kingdom for the sake of the land and for the sake of the animals. With that in mind, the Jeeps used for Kilimanjaro Safaris run on liquid propane, which helps keep emissions low.

10. **Pangani Forest Exploration Trail:** They aren't a secret and they aren't really hidden, but most guests don't notice the Herpetology Field Notes along the trail. Take a look; they make for interesting reading.

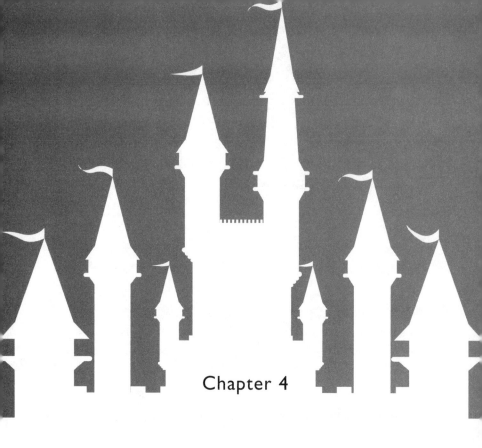

Chapter 4

Disney's Animal Kingdom

Jambo! Welcome to Disney's Animal Kingdom, where the most important word to remember is NaHTaZu. You'll hear it a lot, this splendid word of wisdom. If you want to know what it means, say it quickly. Did you get it? If not, pronounce it like this: Not A Zoo!

Remember that word, because Animal Kingdom most certainly is not a zoo. It is first and foremost an adventure, a story in which you must choose your path right from the start. Will you go this way? Will you go that way? When you reach a divide—and there will be many on this journey—which road will you choose, and where will it lead? No matter which direction you take, the message here is clear: Observe and appreciate the intrinsic value of nature. The beauty of the living world surrounds you, but beware there is an unmistakable element of danger around every corner, too!

Just as nature evolved on the strength of predator and prey locked in their timeless battle, so, too, does the park evolve, giving rise first to vast expanses of lush vegetation, then celebrating beasts and bugs of every variety, and finally, incorporating the human element. But there is innocence here as well, and a sense of cooperation as humans and animals strive to find a balance. Most times, they succeed; occasionally they don't, and the story of their struggle bursts to life as the park unfolds around you.

In direct opposition to every other theme park in Orlando, the slower you take your day at Animal Kingdom the more you will see, so a second important word to remember while touring here is *meander*. A deliberate, appreciative wander will reward you with visual delights around every corner, tucked into every landscape, and over every bridge. The animals are, literally, everywhere! Some are real; some are not—but all hold unending fascination for those who take the time to look.

Imagine That!

Many creative minds worked together to bring Disney's Animal Kingdom into being, but the lead Imagineer primarily responsible for everything you see in the park was Joe Rohde, executive designer and senior vice president of Walt Disney Imagineering. Part modern-day Indiana Jones, part whimsical artist, Rohde began his career with Walt Disney Imagineering in 1980 as a sculptor and painter working on the Mexico Pavilion in Epcot. An avid adventurer, Rohde brings an innate sense of wonder and appreciation of the natural world to his work, with an unerring eye for detail. Rohde and Animal Kingdom are unique in that no other Walt Disney World theme park designated a single designer as the lead Imagineer. As the undisputed expert on the park, we will hear from him several times in this chapter.

Entrance

Animal Kingdom's first secret becomes obvious before you even enter the park. See that tall, thin tree that rises up to the left of the parking lot? It's a cellular phone tower, a necessary encroachment that looks out of place on its own but blends in (at least, a little bit) when made to look like part of the landscaping. You can see it best after you pass through the toll gate, before you actually reach the parking lot.

To avoid wandering the parking lot in a frustrated daze at the end of the day, guests are encouraged to remember their parking section by its animal designation: Giraffe, Butterfly, Dinosaur, Peacock, or Unicorn. The Unicorn section is a throwback to the original plans for the park, which included a **Beastly Kingdom** section, filled with mythical animals. Dragons and unicorns were intended to figure heavily, and you'll see them scattered around the park, on signposts, park logos, and even on the ticket booths.

Imagine That!

When considering the entrance for Animal Kingdom, the Imagineers came up with several creative options. Imagineer Joe Rohde states, "We know that we want to bring people into this park in some way that is different than the way they have gotten into the other parks, which are about human stories and are very architectural environments." Some of the early concepts, as described by Rohde, involved an ark entrance (too controversial), animals marching into the park (too many backsides pointing at guests!), a woodsy art nouveau village with little cottages (too hippie), or a huge, cavernous grotto (too much cement). The grotto idea became the launching point, finally evolving into a lush oasis with small cavern-like coves.

The ground under your feet holds a secret, too, and it starts just after you exit the tram. Those long, wavy red and green patterns imbedded in the pavement form a **giant mural** of sorts. If you follow one of the flowing imprints, you may get the idea it's the branch of a tree, and you'd be right. The green pattern represents the Tree of Life, captured in cement. Can't quite make it out? Google-Earth it when you return home! Even easier, look at the park map.

Take a look at the far-left ticket booth as you pass through the courtyard heading toward the turnstiles. One of your first glimpses of the never-realized Beastly Kingdom can be found here, in the form of a **dragon's head** situated in the center of the building's upper ornamentation.

The Oasis

Disney's Animal Kingdom follows a subtle evolution, beginning in the lush surroundings of the Oasis. There are no rides here and very little evidence of human impact on the environment, animal tracks crisscross the pavement, and there is a distinct and deliberate lack of human footprints. This is the world prior to the dawn of humankind, a peaceful haven before civilization sets in.

Many Animal Kingdom secrets are hidden around the bends and turns of the Oasis. Sometimes they are obvious in all their glory, and sometimes they are so hidden guests are forced to agree that ItzNahTaZu if there are no animals to be seen. But be patient. Instead of rushing off to the nearest attraction, take your time wandering through the Oasis, and you may be rewarded with a glimpse of a military Macaw, resplendent in its emerald plumage, or the elusive Reeves' muntjac, with their delicate hooves and tiny antlers.

Animals move at their own paces, and the Oasis encourages you to follow suit. You may have noticed you are walking up a slight incline as you wind your way through the environment. The gentle hill you are climbing is intentional, quietly prompting you to slow your steps and immerse yourself in nature's splendor.

✳ Fascinating Fact

The original concept-name for the Oasis was Genesis Gardens. However, it was deemed to have religious overtones and was changed to the more descriptive and less controversial title it holds today. ✳

One of the most charming elements in the Oasis tends to become very attached to guests, with comical results. Look for **Wes Palm,** the Talking Palm Tree, who roams around the Oasis most mornings, though occasionally he can be found at the entrance before you pass through the turnstiles. Wes may be potted, but that doesn't stop him from chasing guests he's particularly attracted to and engaging them in conversation, sometimes at great and hilarious length.

A major theme in Animal Kingdom is conservation, with an emphasis on environmental awareness, not only in the park but also on a global level. One testament to Disney's dedication to recycling can be found right under you when you take a seat. All of the benches in Disney's Animal Kingdom are made of **recycled milk jugs**. The napkins you receive with your meal are made from unbleached paper, further protecting the environment from unnecessary pollutants. Although the park had no straws at all until 2008, the paper version now handed out with drinks acknowledges guests' preference for the familiar while providing it in a form that won't harm the animals or the environment.

The Oasis offers an easy opportunity to see one of the **invisible barrier** methods used to keep the animals safely in their habitat. Standing as close to an enclosure as possible, look for the thin metal spokes sticking up in bunches of three. They blend seamlessly with the environment if you are not looking for them, but they are effective barriers that do not harm the animals in any way while maintaining a natural look inside their living environment.

Discovery Island

Discovery Island was originally the name of an 11½-acre island on the southeast shore of Bay Lake near Magic Kingdom, a perfect little paradise where guests could get up-close and personal with free-roaming birds, tortoises, and small mammals. When Disney's Animal Kingdom opened, the area of the park now known as Discovery Island was called Safari Village. Because of the park's popularity, Discovery Island's attendance suffered, and sadly, the island closed in

1999 and the name was given to the beautiful area surrounding the Tree of Life. The greeting here in Discovery Island is "Viva Gaia," meaning "Live long, Mother Earth."

The Tree of Life is an awesome achievement, standing 145 feet tall, carved with 325 reptiles, mammals, and birds, all designed to take your breath away the instant you walk from the Oasis into Discovery Island. The bridge between the two areas is wide in recognition of the fact most guests will stop dead in their tracks when they see it. While the view from here is astounding, one to be savored slowly as your eye travels across its 160-foot expanse for the full impact, it is even more incredible seen up-close, and you will get close enough to touch its roots in just a moment. Have cameras at the ready; your journey takes you underground shortly.

✳ Fascinating Fact

When sculpting the animals on the Tree of Life, artists had only between six and ten hours to finish each animal completely. Any longer than that and the plaster was too firm to work with. ✳

Whether the jaw-dropping sight of the Tree of Life brings guests to an abrupt halt or they are too busy rushing off to Kilimanjaro Safaris to see much of anything, most people never make it to **Discovery Island Trails** for one of the best-kept secrets in the park. Take that first photograph of the tree from the walkway, but then walk to the back of the trails for an even more magnificent view, with no obstructions and no unwanted passers-by in the foreground of your pictures. If you arrive first thing in the morning or return toward the end of the day, it is likely you will have the area to yourself.

If ever there was a time to be glad for long waits, it's while you're winding your way toward *It's Tough to Be a Bug*. Even better, head underground and enjoy the **Tree of Life's roots** when there are relatively few guests in the queue. This has to be one of the most visually rewarding places in any Disney park, a masterpiece of storytelling in its own right. Just as the building blocks of life brought forth simple forms at the outset, becoming more complex as life took hold and the full kaleidoscope that is the animal kingdom literally branched outward, so, too, do the roots of the Tree of Life unfold their evolutionary story.

As you begin your journey through the roots, the first carvings you encounter are dinosaurs and prehistoric sea life (look up to see the pterodactyl flying above you). Next, you'll encounter African wildlife, then birds, and then bugs. The farther along the path you are, the more complex and varied the carvings become. Look up, look down, turn around, and look back—life surrounds you!

With that progression in mind, can you find the **grizzly bear**? He is worth seeking out, so keep him in mind as you wind your way through the roots.

✳ Fascinating Fact

When Animal Kingdom opened, many guests wondered if there were any animals in the park. Sightings were "disappointing" so the Imagineers had to find ways to coax reclusive residents out into the open to enhance the guest's experience. Using the "you can lead a horse to water" theory, they created landscaping that held a certain appeal to the animals—a watering hole, a feeding opportunity, or a cool spot on a hot day—while maintaining a natural look within the environment. Many of the stumps, trees, rocks, water features, or reed beds you see may actually be a feeding station or an air conditioner, attractive features for the wildlife resulting in better viewing opportunities for guests. ✳

As you get closer to the entrance for *It's Tough to Be a Bug*, and also once you are inside the lobby, notice the clever **posters** advertising feature films, such as the soldier termite in Termiteator, the high-thrills flick Weevil Keneevil, and the ever-popular Clair De Room, starring, of course, the Stinkbug.

The last animal you see before you walk through the turnstiles is the chimpanzee, and in this case, a very special chimpanzee. As the Tree of Life was being carved, Jane Goodall, the world's foremost authority on chimpanzees, was invited for a viewing. As the story goes, she asked where the chimpanzee was located and, because chimps were somehow overlooked, a carving of the chimp Jane named **David Greybeard**, the first chimpanzee observed making a tool in the wild (and thus redefining the popular understanding of what it means to be human), now holds a place of honor on the Tree of Life. And he'll hold you, too, so climb up on his lap for a photo. Then, look to your left where you will find a small plaque on the wall telling Jane's story. As an interesting aside, David Greybeard is the only named animal on the entire tree.

Now that you've reached the end of the queue and you're standing in front of the turnstiles, you are probably frustrated at having missed the grizzly bear. Funny you didn't see him, because he saw you. Look over to your right. He was hiding behind the root as you rounded the corner! Cute, isn't he?

Once the show starts, a brilliant piece of Disney Imagineering literally pops right up! The animatronics version of **Hopper** in *It's Tough to Be a Bug* is eight feet tall and is one of the most complex animatronics ever made. Hopper also plays a not-so-obvious role. His sudden, angry appearance signals the beginning of the end for many children viewing the show. When Hopper arrives, cue the crying!

As you exit the show, turn left rather than following the crowds off to the right. A lovely, winding trail affords a spectacular view of the Tree of Life's carvings most guests never see (remember to look up, down, and all around). It also makes for a quiet break from the crowds, especially welcome during the busier seasons, and it is a good shortcut into Africa.

Before you make your way along the path, take a look at this section of the tree. Can you find the **scorpion**? It is actually an Imagineer signature of sorts. Zsolt Hormay, chief sculptor and senior production designer of the Tree of Life, included the scorpion and a cuddly **koala bear** (on the front of the tree) in the design, at the request of his young son and daughter. Can't find them? See Solution 8 in Appendix B.

Also keep an eye out for the **giraffe** carvings. They were placed on the tree in honor of the park's first inhabitants, the gentle reticulated giraffe. Find their likeness just above the scorpion and the owl.

Imagine That!

The Tree of Life concept presented a problem for Imagineers, who originally intended it to have a restaurant and a children's play area inside. Concept drawings included a geodesic dome serving as the canopy portion of the tree, requiring a sturdy support system. As often happens, the challenges led to solutions that changed the entire direction of the idea. Imagineer Joe Rohde recalled, "Very late in the process, one of the engineers came in and said, 'Now that we have designed the steel and the branches to hold up that geodesic dome, those branches would hold up anything. We don't need the geodesic dome because the tree is so strong that we could just hold up the branches themselves.' So we rapidly re-conceptualized the tree to become the tree you see today."

They aren't a secret, but many families overlook the six **Kid's Discovery Club** locations scattered throughout the park. Youngsters ages four through eight are the primary audience, but the young at heart are welcome to participate, analyzing animal tracks and plant scents, identifying objects by touch, excavating fossils, and discovering wildlife you may recognize from your own backyard. What child can resist meeting a real live cockroach, tarantula, or the ever-popular lubber grasshopper?

Don't miss the **Ant Vision viewers** at the Discovery Island location, just outside the exit for *It's Tough to Be a Bug*, and be sure to pick up a Field Guide for collecting a special Conservation Stamp at each Discovery Club location.

To give the Tree of Life an added element of realism, there are **expansion joints** connecting each branch to the trunk. This allows the tree to sway in the wind as nature (and the Imagineers) intended.

Before you leave Discovery Island for adventures beyond, take note of a bit of hidden magic that's right in front of your eyes, though you may not have noticed it. It's clear that each of the gift shops has a nature motif, but did you notice that each of them has (of course!) a specific theme? Island Mercantile's theme involves migrating animals, the animals at Beastly Bazaar all live in or around water, those at Creature Comforts are patterned animals, and Disney Outfitters celebrates animals that live in herds. It's obvious now that you know, isn't it?

Two of the nearby restaurants also got into the act, with the rooms at Pizzafari and pavilions at Flame Tree Barbeque having a **predator/prey** element to them. You're surrounded by one species bent on making a meal of another, and you symbolically become part of the act as you devour lunch or dinner.

Pizzafari, where every room has its own theme, has two more curiosities worth seeing before you head into Dino-Land. There is a small cove in the restaurant, called the Upside Down room. Every animal here has an inverted view of the world, except for one. Look for a little **blue bug** about to be devoured by a bird, on the back wall above the door-jamb. It's the only creature in this room that maintained its upright status. Although the bug's directional focus remains intact, a **possum** hanging from a tree over the door was not so lucky. It isn't intact at all and only its tail remains! Find its comical remnants between three pink possum friends.

Imagine That!

Jim Hill, award-winning author, longtime Disney watcher, and web-master of Jim Hill Media news site, has documented the evolution of the parks, from early concept designs to the final guest experience, with an appreciation for the level of detail that makes Animal King-dom special. "I remember the stories about how Joe Rohde worked so hard to create the entrance to Animal Kingdom, the Oasis, with its little weaving paths. The area is supposed to teach you that this is a different park and that you have to use a different set of skills here. You're going to have to move slowly, observe carefully, and it was going to pay off. Rohde designed the rest of the park like that. If you go down into the Discovery Island Safari Village Area and look at the wood carvings on the outside of those buildings, they brought in all these Indonesian wood carvers and they did amazing work."

DinoLand U.S.A.

Pass under the Olden Gate Bridge (groan!) and the world of dinosaurs opens up in front of you. You're not actually visiting during the time of the great beasts though. Instead, you're working with a group of scientists and student paleontologists who have unearthed a treasure trove of fossils. But there is a distinct feeling that the two groups may not be completely in harmony. For the students, it's all about fun. The scientists, however, are on a serious mission, and the divide in their territory (and in their thinking) is symbolized by the changes in the pavement. The area's red pavement is the realm of the scientists; the dirt-like pavement is the paleontologists' stomping ground and the location of their dig sites.

The Boneyard

One of the first areas you come across after you pass under the Olden Gate Bridge is the Boneyard play area, a great place to let children loose while adults take a much-needed break. But even the most tired tourists will find some of the Boneyard's hidden secrets entertaining enough to get up off their crates and take a look (or a listen). And speaking of crates, there are **two large boxes** just after you enter the Boneyard, on the left side next to the stairs, which make great rest spots while the young'uns play. But don't sit down yet. Lift the lid on the second crate, and you'll hear something scurrying around in there! Lift it again (and again) for variations on the theme.

Off to the right near the Jeep in the Boneyard, you'll see a rock formation with rib bones showing through the strata.

Go ahead and push on each one. You've found the musical **xylobone**.

Go around the corner to the left of the xylobone, if you're eager to follow in the tracks of some of Earth's biggest reptiles. Step on the **footprints** embedded in the ground and you may hear a growl, a trumpet, or a roar erupt from the caves behind you.

The scariest thing you're likely to see in the caves, however, are grown men wearing socks with their sandals. But an interesting detail illuminates the pathway for scrambling youngsters. The light inside the caves is provided by **flashlights** left by exploring fossil hunters.

You wouldn't expect to see a tiny stairway leading up to a miniature door carved into the rock while you're exploring for dinosaur bones, but there it is, in the rock formation to the left of the dinosaur tracks, which begs the question: What's back there? Go ahead . . . **open the door**. I dare you.

Seek out the picnic table inside the Boneyard, usually located toward the front by the two yellow slides. The students can't resist carving their thoughts into the table. If you look closely, you will also see some **dinosaur prints** on one of the benches.

Next, take the stairway up to the second level after you pass the picnic table. There is a small area near the entry to the red, blue, and yellow tube slides, where the students base themselves during digs. Check out some of their **paraphernalia** and the funny comments on the blackboard where their work schedules are posted.

Dinosaur fossils aren't the only treasure in DinoLand. Tacked to the upper right-hand corner of the bulletin board just across the pathway from the Dig Site is a **hand-drawn map of DinoLand** as it existed when the park first opened.

The Fossil Preparation Lab and Dinosaur Jubilee (formerly a walk-through exhibit featuring casts of dinosaur skeletons and artifacts) are now extinct, replaced by an enormous yellow "concreteasaurus" and the Primeval Whirl. The ride **Countdown to Extinction** became a somewhat tamer version of itself and was renamed Dinosaur! to coincide with the release of the movie of the same name in 2000.

Check out the **advertisements** on the bulletin board, just above the bench. Among the ads is one from the museum's director, Diana Sore (*groan!*), who is looking for a head researcher at the Dino Institute. Dr. Dunn needs someone to house-sit, and an unidentified SWF (single white female) is looking for a SM (single male) to break her "three month monotony"; funny little additions that enhance DinoLand's storyline.

Each area in Disney's Animal Kingdom has been landscaped with plants found in the land's corresponding part of the world. Even DinoLand looks as ancient as it is supposed to be, with the addition of monkey-puzzle trees, ferns, and twenty species of magnolia whose ancestors date back to the Cretaceous period. Another fun fact to bear in mind as you tour is every bone you see is a cast of a real fossil.

Take a look at the **Dino Institute Schedule** posted in the lower right-hand corner of the bulletin board. It's an easy life when you're a student paleontologist, with only one task between meals: breakfast, dig, dig, dig, dig, dig, lunch, dig, dig, dig, dig, dig, dinner.

Before you move on, take a quick look just above the bulletin board at those funny shapes between the top of the board and the roof. Do they look vaguely familiar? They're **dino vertebra**, strung like an abacus.

It isn't a secret, but it might as well be since most guests pass right by the live **American crocodile** that makes his home between the Dig Site and Dino Bites. As you leave the Dig Site area and walk toward Restaurantosaurus, give him a wave and a smile as you walk past and consider this: his largest ancestors were as long as a *T. rex*!

✳ Fascinating Fact

Did you know the crocodile takes its name from the Greek words kroko (meaning "pebble") and deilos (meaning "worm")? I dare you to look him in the face and call him a Pebble Worm! Even more fascinating, his closest living relative is the modern bird. ✳

Restaurantosaurus

It's not a ride, but it certainly is an attraction. Restaurantosaurus is filled with fabulous little gems that make DinoLand feel like a real working environment, but it does have at least one foot in reality. You can't miss the big silver **Airstream travel trailer** sitting right outside the restaurant which, in real life, belonged to the grandmother of one of the park's Imagineers.

If you look at the roof of the restaurant before you enter, you'll see that the student paleontologists bunking down in the attic of the Restaurantosaurus are definitely out to cause trouble. They have been taking potshots at the **water tower** from a lawn chair on the roof of the restaurant.

Even if you have already eaten, be sure to visit the restaurant to see what the students have been up to. It's hard to say where they got the **dinosaur-head** trophies to the left of the food counter, but it's pretty obvious why the dinosaurs became extinct, since one of them still has a French fry box stuck to his lip! And if you line your camera up just right, so that the antlers above it appear to sit on the dino's head, you'll have photographic evidence of the only known carnolope on record (okay, *you* come up with a good name for a dinosaur with antlers).

Below the dino-head trophies, you'll see a **bulletin board** with humorous news items. Apparently Dr. Helen Marsh, director of the Dino Institute, seen in the pre-show movie for Dinosaur!, has a subscription to *Discover* magazine. Talk about attention to detail and a commitment to fleshing out the backstory!

Head around the corner to the opposite side of the dino-head trophy wall and you'll find a genuine treasure of Disney memorabilia. A set of **four pen-and-ink drawings** from the 1940s Disney film, *Fantasia!*, in which the drawing's scenes were set to Igor Stravinsky's "The Rite of Spring," depicting the creation of the planet and the rise and fall of the dinosaurs.

Those student pranksters in the Dino Institute Internship Program are at it again, this time covering the walls in the Quonset hut dining area (toward the back right-hand side of the building) with **oily handprints**. At least their handiwork has become an artistic collection of dinosaur murals. You may notice other creative expressions as you peruse the walls.

A quick look around, specifically toward the left-hand window in the Quonset hut, reveals the source of their artistic medium. Although it makes great finger-paint, apparently **Dynoil** is harmful if swallowed and should not be used in Jurassic vehicles. Even though it is made from Completely Natural Ingredients, notice the warning to keep it out of the reach of small mammals (and, I think, budding paleontologists).

On the other side of the restaurant to the right of the food counters, the Bunk Room dining area also houses students who apparently have just done their laundry (look up!). One wonders where they found the time in between pulling pranks on their professors. Look at the **Prank Off** board on the wall across from the upper dorm room, showing the students are clearly winning.

The Hip Joint, just off the Bunk Room, is the place to hang out after a long day of dig, dig, digging. Scattered all over the walls are references to some of the students (really, the Imagineers and workers who created DinoLand), in particular one named Zip and one named Animal. Their favourite jukebox music has a familiar sound but with a slight twist. Listen closely and you'll hear songs you may recognize, all updated with a dinosaur theme.

Just before you enter the Hip Joint, take a look at the **bookshelf** high on the wall to the left of the doorway. The paleontologists are avid readers, with heavy emphasis on all things dinosaur. The classics have spun off into such titles as *Cretaceous Park*, *Captain Cretaceous*, *Dino's in Love*, and Russell Bank's *Rule of the Bone*.

Even the **coffee mugs** haven't escaped the hands of prankster students, as evidenced by the mug on the bookshelf. It belongs to Ann, but *-osaurus* has been added. Looking around, you may notice that suffix is quite popular with the students.

High up on a shelf next to the dining area where the jukebox is located, you'll see a **skull** wearing a hat and sunglasses. Perhaps one of the students spent a little too much time digging in the hot sun.

Exit Restaurantosaurus by the side door across from Dinosaur! and pause a moment to look at the first window on your left. A careless student has left a **dinosaur bone** on the window ledge. Why hasn't it been moved (or stolen)? Go ahead, try to pick it up! It seems to have fossilized to the ledge.

Cretaceous Trail

The mega-thrill ride Dinosaur! is just across the pathway, but before you take your hair-raising journey into the past, take a quick detour over to Cretaceous Trail, just to the left of Restaurantosaurus. It offers a shady break as you stroll though DinoLand, even as it slowly creates a future secret. When Animal Kingdom first opened, the trail's resident **dinosaurs** were an easy-access photo opportunity. Now, they are slowly becoming extinct in the foliage. Look for them while you can; in a few years they may be topiaries!

While you're noticing the landscaping, take a look around for the **monkey-puzzle** tree, similar to the spiky tree you saw in Japan at Epcot. While it wasn't quite a natural fit over there, it certainly feels at home here in DinoLand. The tree's origins can be traced back 60 million years, through fossil records. That's old!

Before you leave the trail, stop for a moment and listen. You can hear the sounds of something big tromping around in there, and if you're very quiet you may be able to distinguish between the real bird sounds and the manufactured ones.

Dinosaur!

It's pretty hard to miss a 40-foot long, 20-foot high meat-eating Tyrant Lizard King, so it is unlikely you will overlook the *Tyrannosaurus rex* charging out of the foliage on the right-hand side of the pathway leading up to the Dinosaur!

attraction. She is an exact replica of Sue, the largest, most complete, best preserved *T. rex* ever found. Sue takes her name from the amateur fossil hunter, Susan Hendrickson, who discovered the bones in South Dakota in 1990, and is a unique specimen in that she was found with a complete breastbone. She is also one of only two *T. rex* fossils discovered with an arm intact. In 1998 Disney's Animal Kingdom received some of Sue's bones, and scientists from the Chicago Field Museum (which made the successful bid at auction for the bones) moved into a fossil preparation lab on public display in DinoLand to begin the cleaning process. The bones were then shipped back to Chicago and Sue now stands proudly (and fiercely) in the Chicago Field Museum's main lobby. Another fascinating fact? Sue's skull alone took 3,500 hours to clean!

Walking through the Dino Institute as you queue for Dinosaur! you enter the rotunda area where it feels as if you have not only gone back in time, you've also gone underground. Strata along the walls give a clue to how far you have traveled into the earth. That dark layer running beside you, about halfway up the wall, represents the **K-T boundary**, the scientific demarcation point between the age of dinosaurs and the age of mammals.

✻ Fascinating Fact

The K-T boundary (K for Kreide, the German name for "chalk," which, translated into English, is Cretaceous, and T for Tertiary, meaning "geological time characterized by the appearance of modern flora and large mammals") is found in a specific strata level in many areas across Earth. Because it has an unusually high concentration of iridium, an element found in greater abundance in asteroids, meteorites, and comets than in Earth's rocks, the boundary is believed by most scientists to be compelling evidence of a meteorite's impact with Earth 65 million years ago. Below the K-T Boundary there is an abundance of dinosaur and other fossils not found in the strata above. At that specific point, at least 75 percent of the species found both on land and in the sea went extinct. According to science, the age of mammals had begun. ✳

If you aren't too frightened about your impending trip back in time, pay attention to the name of the scientist who is about to send you on your search-and-recovery mission. His name is **Dr. Grant Seeker.** (Another groan!)

Because *Dinosaur!* is a popular ride drawing long lines throughout the day, you should have plenty of time to look at the scenery as you wind your way down to your Time Rover. While standing on the stairway just above the loading area, take a look at the pipes running down toward the track. The **chemical formula** painted across the red pipe is the chemical makeup of ketchup, the yellow pipe displays the formula for mustard, and the white pipe is, of course, the formula for mayonnaise. Do you think the attraction's sponsor (McDonald's) may have something to do with this particular secret?

Apparently real-life Carnosauria, of which *Allosaurus*, *Megalosaurus*, and *Gigantosaurus* are examples, aren't considered scary enough when met in a dark prehistoric jungle, prompting Imagineers to create their own Carnotaurus (which, literally translated, means "Meat Bull") with more massive thighs, greater height, and bumpier, knobbier skin. Then, to get around the fact it was no longer a true representation of the species, they dubbed it a new subspecies, appropriately naming him *Carnotaurus robustus*

Floridana. And you're about to encounter him, several times, during your totally terrifying, utterly thrilling journey into the past!

Your knees may be shaking when you exit the attraction, but you can recover from your trip in relative peace and quiet if you take the shady trail between Dinosaur! and Chester and Hester's Dino-Rama, just to the left of the attraction's entrance. Pause for a moment to regain your balance and listen closely for the sounds of dinosaurs in the brush. Then, as you walk toward the shop at the end of the trail, notice how the pavement changes. Remember the **demarcation line** between the scientist's area and the student's archeological site? It's even more obvious along the trail in this area.

Chester & Hester's Dino-Rama

Chester and Hester Diggs, the eccentric proprietors of Chester & Hester's Dino-Rama, are definitely the local yokels, with a sense of style that is seriously kitschy! But they do know a great opportunity when they see one. They turned their little plot of land into Dino-Rama, a garish roadside carnival, after their dog unearthed a bone that turned out to be a dinosaur fossil. The Diggs saw dollar signs, refusing to sell their land when the Dino Institute caught wind of the geological treasure-trove beneath their feet, instead adding to their empire with Dino-Rama.

Every good road site attraction has its gift shop, and you'll enter Dino-Rama's just past the shady trail you took from Dinosaur! Chester & Hester's Dinosaur Treasures recalls the tacky roadside souvenir shops dotted across America, and some would say, still prevalent in the Kissimmee / Lake Buena Vista area today. There is an awful lot to look at here, but pay particular attention to the **photograph** on a shelf on

the left side in the center of the store. It shows Chester and
Hester in all their glory, and it also holds a bit of a secret.
There's something a bit odd about them, isn't there? Can
you figure out what it is? Give it a shot, then look at Solution 9 in Appendix B.

You can't miss Dino-Rama's main attraction, just outside Dinosaur Treasures. Primeval Whirl packs a real punch,
and it's Chester and Hester's less costly time-travel answer to
Dinosaur! But it also pays homage to another Walt Disney
World attraction. See those three **dinosaurs hitching a ride**? Do
they remind you of another Disney classic? If you thought of
Haunted Mansion's hitchhiking ghosts, you'd be right!

Turning to your left as you exit the gift shop (or to the
right if you are near TriceraTop Spin), you will see a large,
stylized dinosaur, apparently cobbled together by Chester
and Hester with various bits of debris and concrete. Stand
facing the dinosaur's left side and look for the small gold
pin, just below the fourth scale on his back. That's a Cast
Member's **one-year pin**, awarded after a year of service.

As you walk toward the fun-fair games, take a look at
the pavement. Evidence of the area's original use can still
be seen, in the form of white **parking space** lines. Chester
and Hester built their roadside carnival on what was once a
parking lot, perhaps taking their cue from the thousands of
temporary carnivals that spring up in parking lots all over
the United States during the warm weather months.

Before you exit Dino-Rama and head past the giant
orange "concreteasaurus" toward Asia, pay attention to
Highway U.S. 498, which runs around the carnival, creating a subsection of sorts within DinoLand. Exit toward the
Boneyard play area, taking note of the hedges, which spell
out the name of the area, boarded in **license plates** from dif-

ferent states across the nation. Highway U.S. 498 is also a reference to the opening date of Disney's Animal Kingdom—April 1998.

There is no themed greeting in DinoLand, but there are a few **themed farewells**. When you leave the area, be sure to say, "Rock On!" or "Dig ya later!" to one of the Cast Members.

✱ Fascinating Fact

The Disney / McDonald's / Coca-Cola triumvirate was a strong one. Coke had been supplying soft drinks in the Disney parks since 1955, and McDonald's, the sponsor of DinoLand, established a ten-year alliance with Disney in 1997. Curiously, Coca-Cola is also the soda of choice at McDonald's fast-food chain, and Disney often slips a small toy into children's Happy Meals when promoting their latest, greatest feature film. Just to complete the trinity's union, when Animal Kingdom opened in 1998, Coke bottles carried the AK logo, as they have done for various Disney grand events ever since. ✱

Asia

Welcome to Anandapur (pronounced "Uh-NON-duh-pour") the "place of delight"! As its name implies, enchantment awaits at every turn, capturing the essence of Asia in minute detail. The pavement beneath your feet shows an evolution that not only includes the imprint of human feet, but also a great feat in the evolution of transportation. People are not just walking in Asia; they're also riding bicycles, a popular mode of transportation in these parts. However, at the base of the mountains you will only see human prints and hoof prints. You are now too high up for bicycles, and pack animals are the transportation of choice.

✳ Fascinating Fact

Most of the foliage was hand-selected for use in Disney's Animal Kingdom. Some of it, however, was trunk-selected. When collecting seeds in Nepal, Paul Comstock, one of Disney's landscape architects, rode an elephant named Durgha Kali who selected plants with her trunk, picked them, and "handed" them to Comstock. The seeds collected were used to create part of the landscaping we now see in the Africa section at Animal Kingdom. ✳

The small, colorful flags gently flapping above you as you tour Asia are recreations of the **prayer flags**, common in Tibetan culture. They are believed to bring prosperity, long life, and happiness to the flag's planter and anyone in the area. Their icons represent aspects of the enlightened mind rather than representing beings outside oneself. When placed indoors, they increase the spiritual atmosphere within the home; when placed outside, the wind carries their prayers throughout the world. While some traditional prayer flags feature Buddhist symbols and some contain actual prayers, those in Animal Kingdom's Asia have generic icons to avoid being considered religious in any way.

There is a specific order in which the five color flags are traditionally displayed: yellow, green, red, white, and blue (placed left to right or bottom to top). They represent, in order: **earth, water, fire, cloud, and sky**. However, Anandapur does not necessarily adhere to this tradition.

Expedition Everest—Legend of the Forbidden Mountain

Expedition Everest is the attraction that really put Asia (at least, Disney's Asia) on the map. It is your first peek into Animal Kingdom when you reach the parking lot and it is the first attraction you see when you enter Asia from DinoLand. As the park's newest attraction, Everest reaches into the Imagineers' bag of tricks and pulls out every one of them. The theme here is immense, not only in the size of the attraction but also in the amount of detail. You will be climbing up the Forbidden Mountain soon, but for now, slow down and allow yourself to be fully absorbed by the story that surrounds you.

As you think about the name of the attraction, an interesting detail may occur to you right away. Although you are on an expedition to climb Mount Everest, the legend here is really about the **Forbidden Mountain**. The train ride will take you to a base camp on the Forbidden Mountain, where preparations for the ascent will take place. However, there is something standing in the way, and it's a big, angry something!

Imagine That!

The Forbidden Mountain could well be called Mystery Mountain. Because it was essential the designers could see the mountains as they were being built (to preserve scale, forced perspective, etc.), traditional scaffolding could not be used. Instead, the Imagineers came up with the creative idea of toothpick scaffolding. Once in place, over 2,000 toothpicks (steel beams) stuck straight out of the mountain, with flat bases for the builders and artists to stand on as they worked, leaving a near-complete view of the mountain range as it went up. Finally, each toothpick was cut off, leaving no trace of the scaffolding. If an architect in the future were to look at the design without seeing the schematic, they would be hard-pressed to figure out how Everest was built. Another interesting tidbit: In the past, using clay models, it would have taken three years to complete the design for Everest. With today's computer technology, it only took eighteen months.

Your journey up the mountain and into the lair of the Yeti begins in the village of Serka Zong, progressing through Norbu and Bob's booking office for Himalayan Escapes, past the Yeti Mandir, on into Tashi's Trek and Tongba Shop, finally making your way through the Yeti Museum that was once an old tea warehouse, now owned by Professor Pema Dorjay, before you begin your trip into the unknown.

Before you enter the queue, it is worth taking time to notice some of the curious elements outside the ride, such as the **totems** in front of Expedition Everest, which were hand-created by Nepalese woodcarvers. Just as there is a stark contrast between the real totem pole in Epcot's Canada Pavilion and the one designed by Imagineers, so, too, is there an obvious authenticity here. They look, and are, the real deal.

Even if you know everyone in your group is tall enough for Expedition Everest, take a look at the **height ruler** (in front and to the left of the ride entrance) used to confirm children are tall enough to ride. It indicates youngsters must be "one Yeti-foot high" to journey up the Forbidden Mountain.

Symbolism is everywhere, even on top of the buildings. See all that **firewood** on the rooftops? It isn't used for heating or cooking. Wood is scarce high up in the mountains so having a stack of it on your rooftop is an indication of wealth. The more wood you have, the wealthier you are.

No self-respecting Himalayan homeowner would be without a good supply of **yak dung**. Dried, it makes excellent fuel; fresh, mixed with mud, it makes a fabulous building material for homes. The Imagineers did not overlook this architectural anomaly when it came time to build Serka Zong. You may notice the building's unique texture, but happily, you won't notice a smell.

You may also have noticed there is quite a bit of **red coloring** throughout Serka Zong, on the buildings, statues, signs, and other artwork. Red is considered a color of protection, a magic spell of sorts that keeps evil spirits at bay, and the village's inhabitants are paying close attention now that the Yeti has been angered.

Enter the queue and you immediately have a sense that you have truly entered the story. References to the mountain's protector are everywhere. Displayed in cases and on shelves are **statues of the Yeti**, with his hand raised. These statues mimic Hindu and Tibetan god and goddess statues, and in this instance, the Yeti holds the Forbidden Mountain range in his hand, his other hand raised in a warning to turn back. The statues themselves symbolize his status as a spiritual being.

There may not be many flush toilets or high-definition televisions in Nepal, but they do have the necessities of life, such as Coca-Cola. Look for **Nepalese Coke bottles** scattered throughout the queue for Everest. There are also advertisements painted on the walls throughout Anandapur, with the famous white lettering on red background. You may not be able to read the words, but there is no doubt what they mean.

Ready for another "Wow, that's real attention to detail" moment? Look up as you queue through the first building.

See those big lamps hanging from the ceiling? They've been given a second life as lighting for the ride's queue, but they were originally **tea leaf–drying lamps**. In their second life here in Serka Zong, they are in keeping with the building's tea plantation theme.

The standby queue offers a hint of what's to come when you reach the mountaintop. Look for a **tent** on the left-hand side, which obviously caught the attention of the Yeti. The status of its former occupant is seriously in question.

You will see more evidence of wood-gathering as you enter the courtyard while queuing for Expedition Everest. Those **mulberry trees** are rather pathetic looking, with their branches cut short and gnarly bits all over their trunks. They aren't ravaged by disease though, they've been harvested! Villagers cut off the branches and then let them grow again, leaving knobby scars.

If you had the forethought to pick up a FastPass and are now walking through the FastPass queue, take a moment to notice the document hanging to the left of the praying monkey statue in the first office you enter. Renowned mountaineer, author, poet, and conqueror of Everest, Pat Ament's humorous book, *10 Keys to Climbing Everest*, is apparently required reading before making the trek up the mountain. Curiously enough, so is *Walt Disney Imagineering*, written by (who else?) the Disney Imagineers. You'll see a copy of the book in the Anandapur Mountaineering Association shop (the one with all the mittens and hiking gear), on a shelf under a stylized crouching tiger made of wood.

Take note of the **red mark** on the forehead of the Yeti statues (the statues that look a bit like an angry monkey) throughout the line. It is a sign of honor and respect; when the statue is placed in a temple, the red mark also indicates the temple is active and has not been abandoned.

References to the Yeti truly are everywhere (there are 1,000 in the temple alone!). Even the trim along the **Yeti Mandir** (temple) as you round the corner in the queue has a decidedly Yeti-ish look to it, while the artistic planks holding up the eaves show the Yeti fighting off a yak. But that's not the most fascinating fact about this particular temple. The building is an original and was shipped from Nepal, in pieces, to Disney's Animal Kingdom.

Anyone up for a cup of **Ye-Tea**? The Royal Anandapur Tea Company has its own blend, which you will find in a cabinet as you queue through Tashi's Trek and Tongba Shop.

Guests enter the realm of the Yeti aboard the old tea company **steam train**, long abandoned until Norbu and Bob began their Himalayan Escapes tours. The rust-red color of the train cars not only affirm their age, it also serves another purpose. Because the cars look old, they don't need touch-ups (as a shiny car would) when they get scratched as passengers load and unload. Nicks and dents just add to the theme.

While you are waiting to board, notice the boiler at the back of the train. It isn't practical to have a full load of water on board this particular steam train, so Imagineers employed a little magic. Watch closely, and you'll see the **steam** actually comes up through the train from the tracks below shortly before it sets in motion.

It will be difficult to pay close attention to the ride's finer points once you are off on your upward journey, but if you are eagle-eyed and look quickly just before you make your escape past the enraged Yeti, you'll see he has **dirt** around his toenails.

* Fascinating Fact

The Yeti is a temperamental beast, prone to refusing to act his part at times. Rather than giving him a day off or a long lunch break, the attraction attendants deal with his refusal to move in a creative way. They don't shut down the ride, they just turn on a strobe light and blow a fan over his fur when the Yeti stops working, which makes him look as if he's moving. *

As you exit the attraction, dazed but unharmed, your newfound appreciation for the sanctity of the mountain may inspire you to send up your own prayer of thanks for a safe return. And the place to do it would be the **prayer wall** you see off to the left as you are walking up the stairs to the main pathway. Common in Tibetan culture, carved mani (prayer) stones are often piled up near mountain passes, temples, lakes, and other outdoor areas, providing a sacred place for the faithful to pray.

But the biggest secret of Everest is this: The Yeti *isn't* feared as an evil, destructive creature. He is honored, in every way you have just observed and in real life among the Himalayan people, as the spiritual **Protector of the Mountain**. Sure, he's going to chase you away as soon as you reach the summit, causing your train to careen wildly down the mountain. But hey, he's only doing his job. You dared to enter the realm of the Yeti!

After exiting the Expedition Everest ride (and escaping the inevitable gift shop), the **Anandapur Ice Cream Truck** to the left of Everest as you head deeper into Asia is so outrageous, you just know it has to be something significant. And you're right. Although it now serves up sweet treats, it actually came from Nepal with all but two of the mini murals painted on it, exactly as you see them now. Only the large painting of the siamang apes' towers (to the far left of the service window) and the mural of Kali River Rapids (below the service window) were added once it reached Animal Kingdom.

In reality, Everest is rarely the tallest mountain you see from any location and because it is usually viewed from a distance, closer mountains appear to be larger. With that in mind, Imagineers created a **peekaboo moment** (a quick glimpse of something interesting from other areas in the park) with the telescope you see next to the shrine as you leave the Everest area heading farther into Asia. Look through the telescope and you will see it is focused on the mountain to the right of the highest peak. That's Everest! The highest mountain you see is the Forbidden Mountain, and its placement in front of Everest to give the illusion of height is another form of forced perspective.

The shrine to the right of the telescope isn't a random design, either. The **outline of the shrine** represents the shape of the mountain range across the lake. Bend down a bit and the shrine will align with the mountains.

It's awfully difficult to paint an entire mountain range, so Disney Imagineers made sure Expedition Everest's color would remain vibrant by using concrete tinted the same integral color as the paint.

Why is there an **Internet café** advertised on the rather ancient looking Gupta's Gear and Shangri-La Trekkers Inn, on your right-hand side as you leave the Everest area? Because as old as it is, Serka Zong has survived into the twenty-first century and Internet access has arrived.

The **Yeti Palace Hotel**, currently in a state of construction alongside Gupta's Gear and the Shangri-La Trekkers Inn, originally served as an advertisement of sorts for the not-yet-open Expedition Everest. It made its first appearance when the Yeti Palace Hotel was the last thing you reached as the pathway connecting the Everest area to Asia was still being laid down. Everything beyond it was blocked off, but the sign on the wall promised an **Opening Next Season**, which is exactly what Expedition Everest did.

As you leave Serka Zong near the Shangri-La Trekkers Inn and Internet Café, look to your right. That boulder has eyes! Although they are not an exact replica of traditional **Buddha Eyes** (or, Wisdom Eyes), common on Buddhist shrines in Nepal, they're a pretty close representation. Traditional Buddha Eyes also contain a symbol where the nose would be, that signifies the unity of all things, and that element is missing here, indicating they're more a curiosity than a religious symbol.

Another symbol you will find all around the Asia area of the park are the trees Imagineers dubbed Tiger Trees. You will recognize them by the flowing, ragged **ribbons** tied to their branches. Each ribbon represents a passer-by's prayer, and Asian cultures believe those prayers are carried by the wind. You may also notice **small bells** hanging from the tree. The bells serve two purposes: to ward off bad energy, and to acknowledge prayers that have been answered. Why is the tree called a Tiger Tree? In an effort to avoid its having any true religious significance, the deity to whom these prayers are being sent is the tiger, chosen because no culture on Earth worships the tiger as divine.

Having left Serka Zong, you are heading into the jungles of Asia and the first thing you come across is a temple that has been abandoned, due to a flood that, according to its storyline, occurred during its construction phase. Gibbons and siamangs have taken over and are having a grand old time playing on the ropes and scaffolding left behind by the workers. They also hold a wonderful secret, but you must be in the park early if you want to experience it. Every morning between dawn and 7:30 A.M., the gibbons begin their **territorial vocalizations**. Then between 9:15 and 10:00, the siamang apes return the call . . . loudly! It is an astonishing series of sounds, similar at times to a siren wail, which can be heard as far away as two miles. How do the siamangs do it? They have a throat sac that, when filled with air, can expand to the size of their head!

Another interesting tidbit? Most of the residents in Animal Kingdom are trained to respond to auditory cues, both for their safety and for purposes of maintaining their health care routine. The gibbons here at the temple respond to a cow bell and their neighbors, the siamangs, pay attention to the sound of a clacker.

✳ Fascinating Fact

When a Disney Cast Member is "on stage" in any of the parks, he or she will always be wearing a name badge. However, there is one exception: the animal caretakers at Animal Kingdom do not wear the iconic badge, which proves too tempting for their charges. Instead, they have an embroidered badge sewn onto their shirts. ✳

Kali River Rapids

Kali, the Hindu god who lends her name to the river in Animal Kingdom's Asia, is the goddess of "time and of the transformation that comes with death." She is the ferocious incarnation of the Divine Mother and is believed to create the fear of death in the ignorant while removing that fear in those who seek knowledge. With that little tidbit in mind, are you ready for a ride down her river?

The queue delights the eye with thousands of authentic artifacts, but pay attention to the sounds as well. At various points you will be able to hear **loggers** cutting trees in the distance, an indication of what's to come on your journey down the rapids.

Many adventurers have gone before you, braving the rapids and returning to tell about it. Look for the **canoe paddles** with names and comments on them, hanging on the walls as you walk through the Kali Rapids Expeditions room. Some of them are really the hidden signatures of the attraction's Imagineers and designers.

In the last building before you reach the walkway to the loading platform, you'll find several paintings depicting the journey down the Rapids. Each painting has a humorous name above it, but look specifically for the one titled *Khatmandoozy*. See that rider dressed in white? He has what looks suspiciously like a **Nike Swoosh** emblem on his jacket.

Those pesky loggers are at it again. Stop for a moment and listen to the **radio** in the office, just before you board your boat. The announcer warns there is illegal logging in the area, giving you some idea of what you will encounter as your raft makes its way through the jungle.

Imagine That!

Realistic environments are a key element in the parks, but one of the main goals is to bring guests fully into the story in ways beyond the visual. Immersing guests in evocative sights, sounds, textures, and scents is of primary importance, as Imagineer Joe Rohde explains,

"It's got to feel like nature, not just look like nature. If you feel the natu-
ralness, then you're going to feel the threat all the more, which is, of
course, the threat to harvest out the value of nature and turn it from
intrinsic value to monetary value. Therein lays the conflict that is at
the source of almost every story at Animal Kingdom."

So you finally got that six-year-old to let go of the **elephant squirt guns** on the bridge above Kali River Rapids and
you're determined to soak any dry passengers right to their
skin. Now, if you only knew the secret to timing it just right.
Fear not, *Hidden Magic* is here to help! If you wait until your
target is a single raft-length away, then push the button, you
should hit the nail on the head (or the rider in the eye)!

Maharajah Jungle Trek

After your harrowing journey down Kali River Rapids,
you're probably ready for a more relaxed adventure along
Maharajah Jungle Trek, which winds its way through the
Royal Anandapur Forest.

The murals and paintings you see along the trek are of
fictional characters, including the various maharajahs that
have made the Royal Forest their hunting, gardening, and
leisure-time grounds, but there are some lovely little gems
scattered along the trek, even in places you might least
expect them.

Themed as a community house, the fruit bat enclosure
has a few interesting secrets. Although it is no secret all the
bats are male (a feature that may be difficult to overlook
if they're facing you with their wings spread wide!), it's a
curiosity to know the auditory cue they respond to when
summoned by their handlers is the sound made by a **dog
whistle**.

When you leave the main room, look to your right and you'll see a series of interesting pictures in the hallway. The **photographs** are of real caves in Asia that were inhabited by bats, though they were not the bats you see here. Even better, the man in one of the pictures with his back to the camera is none other than Animal Kingdom's lead Imagineer, Joe Rohde.

Exit the bat enclosure and take notice of the wall just beyond the bat house. It runs the full length of the Maharajah Jungle Trek, making it the **largest edifice** in terms of area built inside any of the Disney theme parks.

Are you a **Hidden Mickey** fan? If so, you'll find several of them in the murals of the maharajahs along the wall running through the Jungle Trek. Clouds and clothing are a good place to start your search!

> ✳ **Fascinating Fact**
>
> Searching for Hidden Mickeys is a popular pastime at the Walt Disney World parks and resorts. They're everywhere—in the queues, in the landscaping, throughout the rides, and in the architectural elements—so keep an eye out for them as you tour! If you become obsessed with them, there is a even a book on the subject, <u>Hidden Mickeys</u> by Steven M. Barrett. ✳

As you browse the shops before leaving Asia, notice the picture of the **Royal Couple of Anandapur**. Every shop will have one, not only to honor Their Highnesses, but also to show how wealthy the shop owner is. The bigger the picture is, the wealthier the owner.

Another feature you will come across as you make your way along the path is a recreation of something commonly seen in small villages around Asia. The **drinking fountain** surrounded by various pots and pans mimics the tradition of villagers placing their vessels at local water taps, catching the small stream of water that leaks from the spigot. When one pot is full, a passer-by will swap it for an empty one so that everyone gets their share of water and nothing is wasted. How friendly!

✳ Fascinating Fact

Dedication to the safety of the park's wild inhabitants is paramount in Disney's Animal Kingdom. With that in mind, drink lids are not provided with your beverage order and there are no balloons sold anywhere in the park, as they present a choking hazard to the birds and animals. Remember to monitor yourselves and your children and make sure all rubbish ends up in the trash bin rather than in the animals. ✳

Farther along the path toward Africa, you can see a **boat dock** on the waterway (across from Flights of Wonder) that certainly looks as if it should be used for something. In fact, there is a second boat dock that can be seen over the bridge as you cross from the Oasis to Discovery Island. There was originally a gentle journey from one dock to the other when Animal Kingdom opened. But Discovery River Boats were on a countdown to extinction almost from the moment they loaded the first passengers. Long, slow, tedious queues, a seven-minute journey to nowhere, and the fact guests had to disembark at each dock ensured the cruises would soon be a thing of the past. Adding small animal encounters didn't help, possibly because scorpions and tarantulas in Plexiglas boxes are not everyone's idea of cute and cuddly. The boats found brief new life as Radio Disney River Cruises and now perform the function of a modified Character Meet-'N'-Greet on Discovery River, during which you can neither meet nor greet the enthusiastically waving Mickey and Company.

Some of the hidden magic of the park seems like a secret because guests don't know what they're looking at even when they see it. Some details are secretive because guests in their hurry simply do not notice them. But one hidden gem in the Animal Kingdom is meant to be just that, at least at first. In a park filled with lush vegetation and elaborate scenery, it's easy to overlook one of the most creative artistic elements, designed to blend perfectly with its (or should I say, her) surroundings. Only when she moves do guests realize that clinging vine draped over a utility pole or lounging gracefully against a tree is actually **DiVine**, a character actress who looks for all the world like a long-established part of the landscaping. She shows her lovely face only rarely, but for those who notice her she is a rare gem indeed. She can be anywhere, but she is often found at the front entrance or along the path between Asia and Africa, just before you enter Harambe.

Africa

You have finally reached Africa, the cradle of civilization. Hoof prints dot the pathways, leading off into the lush underbrush. Human influence is evident, but there is a sense of cooperation between people and animals, a feeling of balance, with neither overpowering the other. Enter the village of Harambe, the Swahili word for "let us all pull together," and you'll find a bustling settlement full of music, wildlife,

and some fascinating hidden gems. Of all the lands in all
of Walt Disney World, Africa is the one that most closely
resembles the real thing. Every building you see here is an
exact replica of an existing building in Africa, right down to
the cracks and crevices.

Imagine That!

Imagineer Eric Jacobson, senior vice president of Creative at WDI,
describes the meticulous process of moving a concept from rough
idea through to the "cracks and crevices." "We like to say—and we
follow this extensively—it all starts with a story. In everything we do,
we have a story that we're following so that the entire team knows
what the goal is and what story we're telling. Then, all of that layer-
ing from the initial outline to the script to the physical building to all
the detail supports the storyline that we developed in the beginning.
We may modify it or massage it along the way, but basically we all
follow that one path. Just by doing the detail and those extra things,
it brings the story to life in a way that people really appreciate."

The time period is post-British rule, with evidence of
the occupation (such as the iconic British **phone booth** near
the restrooms across from Tusker House) and of East Africa's
subsequent freedom. Take note of the directional sign next
to Tamu Tamu Refreshments as you approach Harambe, and
in various other locations around the village. The date you
see on the sign's base, **1961**, signifies the year the Republic of Kenya began its road to Independence, when Jomo
Kenyatta won the presidency of the Kenya African National
Union. That date ties Disney's fictional Harambe to Kenya's
real town of Harambee. But another important event took
place in 1961, too. Tanganyika (later called Tanzania) in
East Africa became fully independent of British rule on

November 1, 1961. Because Animal Kingdom's Africa is a blending of many African nations, that political change is also relevant, and is honored through the motto **Uhuru**, the Swahili word for "freedom and unity," which you may find in various locations throughout Harambe.

Strolling around Harambe, you will notice **white bricks** peeking through the pavement, which are meant to be the outlines of a former fort's walls, further indications of past British occupation.

Outdoor **public showers** are common in Africa and the Dawa Bar boasts two, just off to the left near the wall overlooking the river. Go ahead . . . hand your camera to someone else, stand under a showerhead, and pull the rope! I don't really have to tell you what will happen, do I?

Take a short stroll behind Dawa Bar and peer over the edge. It seems someone has taken refuge during their interrupted journey down the river, possibly because their progress was impeded by those cannons located on the fort.

You may not notice anything particularly intriguing about the Hoteli Burudika, just past Dawa Bar as you walk toward Kilimanjaro Safari, but take a look anyway. See that notice posted on the wall with the peculiar word **Jorodi** on it? Say it slowly. It's a hidden Imagineer signature, and by now you can probably figure out whose! Some of the other signs also refer to Imagineers who helped design Animal Kingdom.

Tusker House, just to the right of the Hoteli Burudika, serves up the most imaginative lunch and dinner buffet in any of the Walt Disney World theme parks, making it the perfect dining spot during your day in the park. Whether you have a meal here or not, head out to the patio at the back of the restaurant. You may notice the sounds coming from the **small apartment** on the second floor of the rear building. There is a woman inside, sweeping, doing dishes, sometimes singing softly to herself. If you listen long enough, you may hear her accidentally drop a plate on the floor.

Remember the **sausage tree** gourds in the outpost at Epcot? The tree, properly known as the *Kigelia pinnata*, is native to South Africa and is growing near Mombasa Marketplace and Ziwani Traders. The heavy, woody fruits grow up to three feet long, so they must be trimmed back to avoid them hitting distracted guests as they walk past.

Kilimanjaro Safaris

There is no mistaking Animal Kingdom's message of conservation as your safari takes you out into the African savannah, and the power of being directly immersed in the animals' natural habitat brings that message home in a real and immediate way. Although the environment is closely controlled in some ways, this is one of the few attractions in Walt Disney World where almost anything truly can happen. You never know where the savannah's residents might be at any given time and you never know what you might see. Every journey is different, and in this place, the animals dictate where the magic will be found.

Imagine That!

Kilimanjaro Safaris presented a unique problem for the Imagineers, who recognized the unpredictability of the show environment. Designer Joe Rohde describes how they dealt with the challenge: "Unlike a scene in a ride where you can direct people to 'look over here,' we knew two things: one, you can look wherever you please, and number two, we will never know where the focal object is going to be, which is an animal. The animal could be anywhere and you can look anywhere. So when we did our storyboards, we drew a line on the ride track estimating the average speed of the vehicle, made a dot every thirty seconds, and we drew one-hundred-and-eighty-degree storyboards that we would hold up in front of our faces and go, 'Okay, that's at second number seven hundred, we're here, seeing something like this.' The wildebeests might all be over here, they might all be here, but they're going to be in this scene. We'd pick up the next one, bend it around our head and, all right, this is the next scene. So we could get some sense of what is this going to be like to progress through this environment because, of course, back then we couldn't do a digital ride through. No such thing existed."

Environmental protection is of the utmost importance at Animal Kingdom for the sake of the land and for the sake of the animals. With that in mind, the Jeeps used for Kilimanjaro Safaris run on **liquid propane**, which helps keep emissions low.

While you are out on safari, you may notice the grass is brown rather than a lush green, but it isn't a matter of neglect, it's a matter of design. **Natural grasses** have a cycle of growth and decline, both in Orlando and in the savannahs of Africa. Happily, Florida's climate does occasionally mimic Africa's in that regard, saving the landscapers the job of making the grass dry out for a more natural look.

Although many of the animals you see on the safari are able to roam freely, there is actually a certain measure of control to limit their wanderings. Guests cannot see the deep moats, hidden dividers, and other **human-made boundaries**, which helps maintain the feeling of being completely "out in the wild."

For the animal's safety, many of them must return to a shelter for the night. How do they know when to return? As you now know, each species responds to a specific sound. Out on the savannah, zebras return when they hear a cowbell, giraffes return to the sound of a sports whistle, most of the hoofed animals respond to a horn, and the Thomson's gazelles have the most unusual signal—they come running when they hear a goose call. ✳

Most of the landscaping throughout the savannah is real, but some of it is not. The termite mound, giant baobab tree, and those enormous ostrich eggs are less about the natural process and more about convenient engineering.

For the enjoyment of passengers, your driver will tune into music on the Jeep's radio, which plays an uplifting, inspiring tune. It is a composition called "Hapa Duniani," incorporating a modified version of **Baba Yetu**—The Lord's Prayer—in Swahili, as sung by the Voices of Celebration. Beautiful!

There is more to explore, this time on foot. Your next adventure waits just around the bend, to the left of the exit for Kilimanjaro Safaris, in the form of a walking path that was originally known as Gorilla Falls Exploration Trail. The name changed shortly after the park opened, but the peaceful respite from Africa's hustle-bustle remains.

Pangani Forest Exploration Trail

Pangani, a small town in Africa in the Republic of Tanzania along the Indian Ocean coastline near the border with Kenya, was once an active center of trade but is now a peaceful retreat, as it is here in Animal Kingdom. Walk the

Pangani Forest Exploration Trail for a view of something secretive, if not actually a secret. If you arrive early in the morning or late in the day you may be rewarded by near-empty paths, meaning you will have the reclusive gorillas all to yourself. The quieter you are, the more likely it is you will see them.

As you wander the path, you'll come across an **archway** that is, literally, a piece of Imagineer handcrafting. The simple mud structure became a work of art when the designers applied their bare hands to the job, each leaving their prints on the arch as they applied its rough surface. Even Executive Designer Joe Rohde and Concept Architect Tom Sze left their imprints on the walls, re-creating a timeless building technique while adding their own silent signature to the work.

They aren't a secret and they aren't really hidden, but most guests don't notice the **Herpetology Field Notes** along Pangani Forest Exploration Trail. Take a look; they make for interesting reading.

Keep walking along the path and you will come across a scientific research station with a small animal whose name is ridiculously comical, especially for the twelve-and-under crowd. The **naked mole rat**, pink and hairless, isn't pretty, but it's a fascinating creature just the same. They communicate through a vast repertoire of whistles and chirps, their sole mission in life is to serve their queen, and they use their buck teeth—which can move independently of each other—to dig tunnels and, to the delight of young viewers, subterranean toilets. But the most fascinating fact of life of a naked mole rat is that they are the only cold-blooded mammal on Earth.

Imagine That!

Some areas of the park are intended to be dynamic, full of action and excitement. Other areas compel guests to take their time and pay attention to the park's real message, as Imagineer Joe Rohde describes, "I think the value is in slowing down and enjoying relationships with the animals, if guests take time to observe them. It takes so little time. If you wait forty-five seconds instead of ten, an animal is going to walk around that bush, and walk over here, and then he's going to walk away. And then forty-five seconds later he's going to walk over here. But if you stay for three seconds, you're going to miss all of that."

Rafiki's Planet Watch

Arriving at Rafiki's Planet Watch, the focus turns to the synergy of the natural world, eventually including humans in that equation. As you walk toward the main building, notice how the **animal engravings** in the pavement demonstrate this sense of working together. At first, each animal is independent from the others; then as they progress further into the area, they come together as a cooperative community. Finally, the large circular engraving shows (literally) how all creatures are inextricably entwined.

Kilimanjaro Safaris and Pangani Forest Exploration Trail allowed the animals to tell their own tale, but here at Rafiki's Planet Watch, the focus turns to what humans can do to keep the scales balanced. Notice the enormous **mural** at Conservation Station. Each animal looks directly at guests, signaling their quiet expectation of human respect and assistance in the natural world's survival.

The trains used to shuttle guests to Rafiki's Planet Watch were built by the model-railroad firm of Severn Lamb, Ltd., at Alcester, England, not far from William Shakespeare's Stratford-on-Avon cottage.

Remember our good friend Wes Palm, the talking palm tree? He's a real charmer, but his heart is true to his long-distance girlfriend, **Pipa the talking recycling bin**, who is sometimes seen wandering around the Conservation Station.

Return to Africa and backtrack to the pathway leading out of Africa toward Camp Minnie-Mickey. You will eventually come across a unique set of lights designed to look like ladybugs. They are the only **ladybug lamps** in the whole park, and they serve as a landmark for Cast Members. First Aid is also located here, and even the most novice CM is fully aware of exactly where to find it, using the ladybug lights as the landmark.

Camp Minnie-Mickey

Formerly earmarked for Beastly Kingdom, this tucked-away land would be a fairly quiet retreat, save for the delighted shouts from children (and children at heart) when they come across their favorite character along the meet-and-greet trails.

Before you reach the junction that takes you into the camp, you'll see the entry to a pathway just across from Pizzafari. It leads down to the roots of the Tree of Life, and there is a charming secret here worth taking the time to explore. When you reach the bend in the pathway, you'll find what looks like a **wall amid the tree roots**. There are several small openings bored into the wall. If you look through them, you get a fantastic view of the tree. Pay special attention to the hole just below and to the left of the uppermost hole. When you peek through it, you have a direct view of a sculpted ant. Why? Because, as the story goes, an ant planted a seed, hoping it would attract more animals. The seed sprouted and grew, coaxing wildlife of all kinds to its shade and to the cool waters surrounding its roots, and when the animals' images reflected off the water, their likenesses magically appeared on the tree!

Look over the right-hand side of the bridge as you cross into Camp Minnie-Mickey. If you think that curious rock outcropping seems to be more than just a natural occurrence, you're right. It's a dragon, turned to stone! It was originally intended to be a dragon-shaped waterfall spewing steam out over the river, but the land it would represent, Beastly Kingdom, was never built.

As you wind your way out of the park at the end of a long, rewarding day, let your pace slow to a meander and pause to enjoy the small details that add an extra element of depth to the stories unfolding around you.

Imagineer Joe Rohde summed it up best when he said, "Just as we hope to bring joy and inspiration to our guests, we hope that they take that inspiration out into the world. See it every day in the living world around them and act upon that inspiration. That is the heart of Animal Kingdom."

Disney's Animal Kingdom Timeline

Forty years after Walt Disney's first theme park in Anaheim, California, opened, the Walt Disney Company announced their intention to build what would arguably be their most unique and challenging park yet. It would take another three years of development, but finally, on April 22, 1998, Disney's Animal Kingdom swung the gates wide and welcomed its first guests.

Attractions open that day were **the Boneyard** dinosaur dig area, **Countdown to Extinction**, **Cretaceous Trail** walking paths, **Discovery River Boats**, **Festival of the Lion King**, **Flights of Wonder** exotic bird show, **Gorilla Exploration Trail**, *Journey into Jungle Book* stage show, **Kilimanjaro Safaris**, **Pocahontas and Her Forest Friends**, **Rafiki's Planet Watch**, and **Wildlife Express**. There were six distinct areas on opening day: the Oasis, Safari Village, Africa, DinoLand U.S.A., Camp Minnie-Mickey, and Conservation Station. A seventh area, Asia, was due to open within a year, with the mythical Beastly Kingdom also on the drawing board.

Beastly Kingdom would cover the "animals of myth and legend" portion of the park, a land of fire-breathing dragons and gentle unicorns; of *Fantasia*'s fauns, centaurs, and dancing hippos; the world of fantasy and fairytale brought to life. It was an incredible concept, but it has yet to be realized.

1998–1999: First Expansion

By the end of 1998, Gorilla Exploration Trail would be renamed **Pangani Forest Exploration Trail**; the Discovery River Boats would close, reopening two months later as **Discovery River Taxis**; and, a month later, Discovery River Taxis would make their final run—sort of. They would reopen in March 1999 as **Radio Disney River Cruise**, a jaunty music and banter-filled boat ride to nowhere (that also closed down before the end of the year, another formula that just didn't work). The March of the ARTimals also paraded for the final time in 1999.

However, there was something new to enjoy, and it was substantial. The new section of Asia opened on April 22, 1999, with the soak-you-to-your-skin river-rafting experience, **Kali River Rapids**, and the peaceful **Maharajah Jungle Trek** walking trail. Kali originally went by the conceptual title Tiger Rapids Run and was intended to showcase animals from Asia as guests floated past in circular rafts. But these things have a way of changing, and Kali River Rapids ultimately became a white-water saturation-fest loosely wrapped around a mild lesson about the dangers of logging.

2000–2001: Time for a Parade

Animal Kingdom sailed along happily for two more years before adding any new attractions. The beautifully artistic **Mickey's Jammin' Jungle Parade** then made its first run on October 1, 2001 (as part of the Walt Disney World-wide 100 Years of Magic celebration), with stylized animal puppets, stilt walkers, and Disney characters riding safari vehicles. The puppets were worn by humans and were designed by Disney's *The Lion King* Broadway show puppet creators, Michael Curry Designs.

There was more on the horizon, though, as Disney was aware there still wasn't enough here to keep eager fans happy and to make it more than a half-day experience in many guests' minds. The first part of it arrived in DinoLand in November 2001, and it finally gave preschoolers a ride tailored just for them. **TriceraTop Spin** was another variation on the Magic Carpets of Aladdin in Magic Kingdom (which were themselves a spinoff of the popular Dumbo ride), but they added a tried-and-true favorite, with baby triceratops ride vehicles instead of flying carpets or big-eared elephants.

2002: Dino-drama

The full development of this new area came in April 2002. **Chester and Hester's Dino-Rama** "roadside carnival" in DinoLand was certainly big all right. At least, the towering yellow brontosaurus framing the entrance was big!

As well as TriceraTop Spin, Dino-Rama consisted of a handful of paid-for carnival games, tacky (intentionally, said Disney) gift shops, and the area's saving grace, **Primeval Whirl**. Though it looked like a cheap (but again, intentionally tacky), "wild mouse" coaster with a cartoonish prehistoric theme, it was actually a dynamic, spinning coaster that packed a gut-wrenching wallop!

Many fans felt the area was the theme park equivalent of "throwing them a bone," no better than the seasonal fairs that spring up all over small-town America. But they still waited for an hour just to ride Primeval Whirl.

2003–2005: A Lucky Strike

Even that wasn't enough to keep guests coming back in droves, as the area was intended to do, since most guests still considered Animal Kingdom a half-day park. But Disney's response was slow. When it did come, in April 2005, it was in the form of a green, cart-toting, free-roaming, self-contained Audio-Animatronic baby brontosaurus with personality plus! Lucky the Dinosaur was a first in Disney's Animatronic world. He could walk on two legs, pulling a cart behind him; he could grab objects in his mouth; he had a degree of vocal expression; and he could fully interact with his "handler" in a most convincing way. However, Lucky's stay at Animal Kingdom was short. By the end of July 2005, he had moved on to Hong Kong Disneyland.

Cries for a new land—ideally, Beastly Kingdom from the park's conceptual stage—grew louder. Although Animal Kingdom had begun to increase in popularity, it lacked the kind of draw that kept guests coming back again and again. But a new day was about to dawn in Animal Kingdom. The Yeti was about to arrive.

2006: Enter the Yeti

On April 7, 2006, **Expedition Everest: Legend of the Forbidden Mountain** careened into Asia with a Himalayan train ride on the fast track toward the mountain's protector, the fearsome Yeti. The coaster's precarious journey put riders face-to-face with the angry beast before making a breakneck escape down the Forbidden Mountain.

Walt Disney Imagineering had a new mega-hit on its hands and had fulfilled, at least to some degree, the park's original intent to include mythical creatures in the animal lineup. Attendance soared.

2007: A Musical Note

Things were going along swimmingly at Animal Kingdom, and on January 24, 2007, a new attraction officially debuted at Theater in the Wild, replacing *Tarzan Rocks*, which closed in January 2006. *Finding Nemo—The Musical* offered a charming human-puppet show featuring Nemo, Merlin, Dory, Crush, and their friends in an artistic pageant the whole family could enjoy.

Because the blockbuster movie, *Finding Nemo*, did not have any songs, adapting it into a musical was left to husband-and-wife team Robert Lopez, co-creator of *Avenue Q*, a Tony Award–winning Broadway hit, and Kristen Anderson-

Lopez, co-creator of a cappella musical *Along the Way,* who wrote fourteen original songs for the new show.

Larger-than-life character puppets were handled by humans dressed in costumes similar to their character, but they were fully visible to the audience. While Disney had employed this technique in Epcot's Tapestry of Nations parade and Mickey's Jammin' Jungle parade, it was unique to an onstage, in-park musical. *Finding Nemo—The Musical* would also mark the first time Disney Creative Entertainment, a division of Walt Disney Imagineering that was created in 2001, produced a major musical show for a Walt Disney World park.

2008: Ten Years After

On April 22, 2008, Disney's Animal Kingdom celebrated its tenth anniversary with a special rededication ceremony featuring renowned primatologist Dr. Jane Goodall, who was there at the beginning of this "new species of theme park" and was happy to mark the park's milestone birthday with her own signature chimpanzee vocalization!

An all-encompassing experience is at the heart of each of the Walt Disney World theme parks. You are meant to participate, becoming part of the story rather than acting as a passive observer. Let *The Hidden Magic of Walt Disney World* inspire you to seek out the finer points and allow yourself to be totally immersed in the heart of the magic.

Appendix A

References

Reference Material

The Imagineers. *Walt Disney Imagineering* (New York, NY: Welcome Enterprises, Inc., 1996).

Walt Disney Media Guide (Lake Buena Vista, FL: Walt Disney World Media Relations, 1998).

Further Reading

For those who would like to add to their appreciation of the Walt Disney World parks, seek out the following:

Barrett, Steven M. *Hidden Mickeys—A Field Guide to Walt Disney World's Best Kept Secrets.*

Brandon, Pam; Meyer, Susan E.; and Lefkon, Wendy. *A Day at Disney.*

Mongello, Louis A. *The Walt Disney World Trivia Book.*

Smith, Dave. *Disney A to Z: The Official Encyclopedia.*

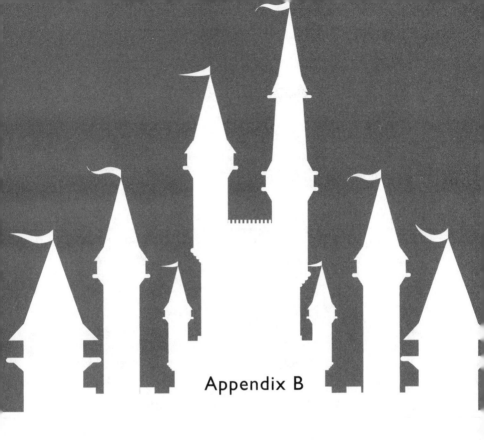

Appendix B

Solutions to Hints

Magic Kingdom

Solution 1: One is on Big Thunder Mountain Railroad, the second is in Carousel of Progress, and the third is in the Toontown Farmer's Market, filled with ice to keep soda and fruit cold.

Solution 2: It's Donald! See his hairs standing straight up? And that is definitely his bill, open in an angry quack, on the right-hand side.

Epcot

Solution 3: The dolphin is on a fountain in the United Kingdom Pavilion, in a small courtyard to the right of the Toy Soldier Shop, just in front of the restrooms.

Solution 4: Mickey is under the striped sail on the Viking ship, toward the left side of the mural. You can see his ears near the mast if you look closely.

Solution 5: Two trolls have found a spot right above the door on the right side of the Stave Church, just above the door; one is hiding on the grassy roof of Kringla Bakeri Og Kafe, near the chimney; two are tucked into the chimney itself; two have found a spot on a ledge to the right of Kringla Bakeri's door; one is perched on a ledge on the right side of Puffin's Roost; one climbed up to the window ledge above the first door to the Fjording (with the running horse sign); two are cuddled up on a windowsill on the right-hand side of the Fjording; three can be found in separate windows on the front of the Fjording's main building (with the green sign); two are huddled together on the rocks to the left of the waterfall; one is peering down at you from a windowsill above the FastPass distribution sign; two are situated in separate windows above Maelstrom's entry; two are hugging each other in a cutout ledge in the rock wall to the right of the ride entry; one is standing on the chimney to the left of Restaurant Akershus; two are in an upper window to the left of Restaurant Akershus, below the steeple tower. That makes twenty-four. Where are the rest? You'll have to exit the main courtyard and head over to the left side of the pavilion. There you'll find one above the left-side entry to the Stave Church; two are on the left corner of the roof to the left of Kringla Bakeri; and one is hiding on the ledge near the roof to the right of the walkway to the restrooms. Fun, hey?

Solution 6: The brown one next to the European trappers shop is the traditional totem pole. The fancier, flashier totem pole is definitely a Disney creation!

Disney's Hollywood Studios

Solution 7: They read, "evil tower U R doomed."

Disney's Animal Kingdom

Solution 8: Find the scorpion on the back side of the tree between the hippo and the owl. Find the koala bear on the front of the tree, tucked behind the eagle's wings.

Solution 9: While no one is sure if Chester and Hester are married, if they are brother and sister, or if they are cousins, one thing is definite: That picture is a split image and the characters Chester and Hester are played by the same person!

Index